Hor

Or
Revisec
Cover
Layout Concept: Klaus Geisler
Picture Editor: Hilary Genin
Managing Editor: Tony Halliday

Berlitz® POCKET GUIDE

Hong Kong

Tenth Edition 2003

Photography by:
Chis Coe/Jon Davison/Walter Imber 20, 25, 28, 39, 41, 42, 46, 51, 53, 55, 56, 58, 64, 68, 78, 81, 83, 84, 85, 86, 89, 90, 91, 95, 96, 97, 100; Dinah Gardner 47, 61, 62, 65, 67, 71, 72, 73, 75; Hong Kong Tourism Board 17, 22, 27, 30, 35, 45, 76, 87; Bill Wassman 6, 9, 10, 18, 26, 29, 31, 32, 36, 37, 38, 44, 48, 52, 54, 57, 98

CONTACTING THE EDITORS

Every effort has been made to provide accurate information in this publication, but changes are inevitable. The publisher cannot be responsible for any resulting loss, inconvenience or injury. We would appreciate it if readers would call our attention to any errors or outdated information by contacting Berlitz Publishing, PO Box 7910, London SE1 1WE, England. Fax: (44) 20 7403 0290; e-mail: berlitz@apaguide.co.uk www.berlitzpublishing.com

Printed in Singapore by Insight Print Services (Pte) Ltd, 38 Joo Koon Road, Singapore 628990. Tel: (65) 6865-1600. Fax: (65) 6861-6438

The Man Mo Temple (page 31) is Hong Kong Island's oldest house of worship

A ride on the Star Ferry (page 23) is the most exciting way to cross Victoria Harbour

The Bank of China Tower (page 25), just one of a glittering array of modern skyscrapers

TOP TEN ATTRACTIONS

In the New Territories (page 45) you'll find plenty of secluded beaches amidst some dramatic scenery

The nine-storey pagoda of Man Fat Tze, the Monastery of 10,000 Buddhas (page 50)

The Tiantan Buddha on Lantau (page 53) is the world's tallest seated bronze statue of the Buddha

Step down a gear on Cheung Chau (page 54), one of the three main outlying islands

Flagstaff House (page 25) is Hong Kong's oldest colonial building, now the Museum of Tea Ware

Day or night, shopping in Hong kong (page 77) is an experience not to be missed

Victoria Peak (page 26) can be ascended by the famous Peak Tram, and provides stunning views over the city

CONTENTS

A ➤ in the text denotes a highly recommended sight

Fact Sheets

INTRODUCTION

Exciting, mysterious, glamorous – these words have described Hong Kong for at least a century. With its vibrant atmosphere and night-and-day activity, Hong Kong is an intoxicating place. There is no doubt that Hong Kong is crowded – it has one of the world's greatest population densities. But it is also efficient, with one of the best transportation systems anywhere, and for such a crowded place, quiet – you don't hear voices raised in anger, motorists sitting on their horns, or loud boomboxes. Shopping never ends – there's always another inviting spot just down the street. You'll find Hong Kong easy to get around, the people helpful, English spoken everywhere, and food that lives up to its reputation.

A New Era

On 1 July 1997 the British Crown Colony of Hong Kong reverted to Chinese sovereignty as a Special Administrative Region of the People's Republic of China. Today Hong Kong remains a capitalist enclave with its laws and rights intact, and China has promised that Hong Kong will continue in this fashion for at least 50 years. Beijing's declared policy of maintaining Hong Kong's prosperity and stability makes sense. Hong Kong has long been China's handiest window on the West, and the city is unrivalled in its commercial know-how and managerial expertise. Around the time of the transition there was much speculation about how things would change. But, in fact, once news of the handover vanished from the front pages, the people of Hong Kong returned to their usual topics of conversation: the economy and the price of housing.

The impression of the visitor today will be that very little has changed. Establishments are no longer preceded by the world 'Royal', Queen Elizabeth has vanished from the coinage, and the Union Jack has been replaced by the flag of China and the new Hong Kong flag with its bauhinia flower. In fact, there have been changes, many of them due to economic progress, new construction and other factors that influence cities all over the world.

Others are more subtle. British social customs are still evident in the kind of polite service you get in hotels and in the long queues of people waiting for buses during rush hour. The British population has decreased; today there are as many American and Australian expats as there are British.

People and Customs

With a population of nearly seven million and a total area of just over 1,095 sq km (423 sq miles), housing is one of Hong Kong's perennial nightmares. To alleviate the problem, the government has become the city's major landlord with the construction of massive residential blocks. Though they have every modern facility, new flats average an internal floor area per person of only around 11 sq m (120 sq ft). Whole cities have been created in the New Territories, although the unimaginative architecture of these towns has been criticised.

Of Hong Kong's population, 98 percent are of Chinese descent. The majority are Cantonese, born in Hong Kong, or from South China, but there are immigrants from all

Fragrant Harbour

Hong Kong's name is derived from the Cantonese phrase for 'Fragrant Harbour' – *Heung Gong*. The evocative name probably derives from the trade in locally-grown incense wood, which once thrived in what is now Aberdeen. Another theory ascribes the name to the bauhinia, an aromatic flower which is native to the region and is now the logo of the Hong Kong administration.

over China. The Chinese people have been described as hardworking and pragmatic, attitudes that have contributed immensely to Hong Kong's success. There are many stories of refugees who arrived with nothing in their pockets, set up a small pavement stall, worked diligently until they had their own shop, and then expanded it into a modest chain.

Exercise on the waterfront

Old customs are still followed: fate and luck are taken very seriously, and astrologers and fortune-tellers do a steady business. Before a skyscraper can be built, a *feng shui* investigation must take place to ensure that the site and the building will promote health, harmony, and prosperity. You'll also notice that gambling is a passion, whether it be cards, mahjong, the lottery, or the horses. Hong Kong has two major racecourses as well as an intensive off-course betting system for punters, and at the weekend the ferries to Macau are crowded with people on their way to the casinos.

What to See

Sightseeing in Hong Kong starts at sea level with the enthralling water traffic – a mix of freighters, ferries, tugs, junks and yachts. Views of the city and the harbour are panoramic. From Victoria Peak, Hong Kong's highest point, or from skyscrapers and hotels, the views are especially exciting at night when the horizon comes alive in a blaze of lights.

The business and financial centre and the soaring architecture are on Hong Kong Island. Across Victoria Harbour, connected by ferry and the MTR underground railway, is the Kowloon peninsula with its hotels, nightlife, and almost non-stop shopping. Beyond, in the New Territories, are a mixture of high-rise suburban towns, ancient sites and walled villages, country parks and farms with ducks and fish ponds. Hong Kong's other, less developed islands, Lantau, Lamma and Cheung Chau, provide getaways. You can also take a ferry to Macau to find an entirely different kind of city, a rare blend of Chinese and Iberian culture.

It's anyone's guess what may happen in the future, but for now Hong Kong bristles with energy and ambition, and for the visitor, this beautiful city with its contrasts and variety is an exhilarating experience.

Despite the gleaming skyscrapers, most of life in Hong Kong is played out at street level

A BRIEF HISTORY

In the popular mind, the history of Hong Kong, long the point of entry to China for Westerners, begins in 1841 with the British occupation of the territory. However, it would be wrong to dismiss the long history of the region itself. Archaeologists today are working to uncover Hong Kong's past, which stretches back thousands of years. You can get a glimpse into that past at Lei Cheng Uk Han Museum's 1,600-year-old burial vault on the mainland just north of Kowloon *(see page 44)*. In 1992, when construction of the airport on Chek Lap Kok began, a 2,000-year-old village, Pak Mong, was discovered, complete with artefacts that indicated a sophisticated rural society. An even older Stone Age site was discovered on Lamma Island in 1996.

The *Hong Kong Story* at the Hong Kong Museum of History is the best way for a visitor to experience the territory's past. For just HK$10, you can travel from a point 400 million years ago to the 1997 handover. Exhibits are richly displayed and include replicas of an 18th-century fishing junk and a 1960s cinema.

While Hong Kong remained a relative backwater in the early days, nearby Guangzhou (Canton) was developing into a great trading city with connections in India and the Middle East. By AD900, the Hong Kong islands had become a lair for pirates preying on the shipping in the Pearl River Delta and causing a major headache for burgeoning Guangzhou; small bands of pirates were still operating into the early years of the 20th century.

In the meantime, the mainland area was being settled by incomers, the 'Five Great Clans': Tang, Hau, Pang, Liu and Man. First to arrive was the Tang clan, which established a

Emperor Kangxi opened trade in Guangzhou on a limited basis

number of walled villages in the New Territories that still exist today. You can visit Kat Hing Wai and Lo Wai, villages with their walls still intact. Adjacent to Lo Wai is the Tang Chung Ling Ancestral Hall, built in the 16th century, and which is still the centre of clan activities to this day.

The first Europeans to arrive in the Pearl River Delta were the Portuguese, who settled in Macau in 1557 and for several centuries had a monopoly on trade between Asia, Europe and South America. As Macau developed into the greatest port in the East, it also became a base for Jesuit missionaries; it was later a haven for persecuted Japanese Christians. While Christianity was not a great success in China, it made local headway, as can be seen today in the numerous Catholic churches in Macau's historic centre.

The British Arrive

The British established their presence in the area after Emperor Kangxi of the Qing Dynasty opened trade on a limited basis in Guangzhou (Canton) at the end of the 17th century. Trading began smoothly enough, but soon became subject to increasing restrictions, and all foreigners were faced with the attitude expressed by Emperor Qianlong at Britain's first attempt to open direct trade with China in 1793: 'We possess all things,' said the emperor, 'I set no value on objects strange or ingenious, and have no use for your country's manufactures.'

Moreover, China would accept nothing but silver bullion in exchange for its goods, so Britain had to look for a more abundant commodity to square its accounts. Around the end of the 18th century the traders found a solution: opium was the wonder drug that would solve the problem. Grown in India, it was delivered to Canton, and while China outlawed the trade in 1799, local Cantonese officials were always willing to look the other way for 'squeeze money' (a term still used in Hong Kong).

In 1839 the emperor appointed the incorruptible Commissioner Lin Tse-hsu to stamp out the smuggling of 'foreign mud'. Lin's crackdown was indeed severe. He demanded that the British merchants in Canton surrender their opium stores, and to back up his ultimatum he laid siege to the traders, who, after six tense weeks, surrendered over 20,000 chests of opium. To Queen Victoria, Lin addressed a famous letter, pointing out the harm the 'poisonous drug' did to China, and asking for an end to the opium trade; his arguments are unanswerable, but the lofty though heartfelt tone of the letter shows how unprepared the Chinese were to negotiate with the West in realistic terms.

'Albert is so amused,' wrote Queen Victoria, 'at my having got the island of Hong Kong.' Her foreign secretary, Lord Palmerston, was not so amused; he dismissed Hong Kong as 'a barren island with hardly a house upon it.'

The Opium Wars

A year later, in June 1840, came the British retaliation, beginning the first of the so-called Opium Wars. After a few skirmishes and much negotiation, a peace agreement was reached. Under the Convention of Chuenpi, Britain was given the island of Hong Kong (where it had been anchoring

Causeway Bay in the mid-1800s

its ships for decades), and on 26 January 1841, Hong Kong was proclaimed a British colony.

The peace plan achieved at Chuenpi was short-lived. Both Peking and London repudiated the agreement, and fighting resumed. This time the British forces, less than 3,000 strong but in possession of superior weapons and tactics, outfought the Chinese. Shanghai fell and Nangking was threatened. In the Treaty of Nanking (1842) China was compelled to open five of its ports to foreign economic and political penetration, and even to compensate the opium smugglers for their losses. Hong Kong's status as a British colony and a free port was confirmed.

In the aftermath of the Opium Wars, trade in 'foreign mud' was resumed at a level even higher than before, although it ceased in 1907. Opium-smoking continued openly in Hong Kong until 1946; in mainland China the Communist government abolished it in 1949.

Commerce and Wealth

The first governor of Hong Kong, Sir Henry Pottinger, predicted it would become 'a vast emporium of commerce and wealth'. Under his direction, Hong Kong began its march towards prosperity. It was soon flourishing; with its natural harbour that attracted ships, Hong Kong leaped to the forefront as a base for trade. Both the population and the economy began to grow steadily. A surprise was the sizable number of Chinese who chose to move to the colony.

In the meantime, the opening of Hong Kong was the last blow to Macau's prosperity. Inroads had already been made

Trading Houses

The Hong Kong of today owes its origins to the big trading houses or *hongs* of the 19th century. It was their top bosses or *taipans* who pressured the British government to secure a base to freely trade their opium and, once acquired, they were the driving force behind shaping the 'barren rock' into a successful trading port. Even today, places in Hong Kong bear the names of these big *taipans* as testament to their early power.

Rival *hongs* such as the Scottish Jardine, Matheson and England's Dent and Company were constantly squabbling among themselves. They were also at loggerheads with the government which was chasing taxes and urging better treatment of the local Chinese. To avoid paying taxes many *taipans* became honoury consuls of foreign powers or sailed their ships under foreign flags.

Many of these *hongs* still exist today, successful because they diversified as Hong Kong's economy changed. Their offices are now hidden in the morass of skyscrapers, their interests spread widely through subsidiaries, and some bought out by Chinese *taipans*. Although they no longer rule the roost, they still wield power from behind the scenes.

by the arrival of the Dutch and Macau's loss to them of the profitable Japanese trade. From then on, until its 1970s comeback with electronic and other export goods, Macau sank into relative obscurity.

Despite the differences between the Chinese majority and the European minority, relations were generally cordial. Sir John Francis Davis, an early governor, disgusted with the squabbling of the English residents, declared: 'It is a much easier task to govern the 20,000 Chinese inhabitants of the colony than the few hundreds of English.'

There were a few incidents: On 15 January 1857, somebody added an extra ingredient to the dough at the colony's main bakery – arsenic. While the Chinese continued to enjoy their daily rice, the British, eating their daily bread, were dropping like flies. At the height of the panic, thousands of Chinese were deported from Hong Kong. No one ever discovered the identity or the motive of the culprits.

Conditions in the colony in the 19th century, however, did not favour the Chinese population. The British lived along the waterfront in Victoria (now Central) and on the cooler slopes of Victoria Peak. The Chinese were barred from these areas, and from any European neighbourhood. They settled in what is now known as the Western District. It was not uncommon for several families and their animals to share one room in crowded shantytowns. So it is not surprising that when bubonic plague struck in 1894, it took nearly 30 years to fully eradicate it. Today in the Western District, you can still wander narrow streets lined with small traditional shops selling ginseng, medicinal herbs, incense, tea and funeral objects.

In 1860, a treaty gave Britain a permanent beach-head on the Chinese mainland – the Kowloon peninsula, directly across Victoria harbour. In 1898, under the Convention of Peking, China leased the New Territories and 235 more islands to Britain for what then seemed an eternity – 99 years.

The 20th Century

The colony's population has always fluctuated according to events beyond its borders. In 1911, when the Chinese revolution overthrew the Manchus, refugees flocked to the safety of Hong Kong. Many arrived with nothing but the shirts on their backs, but they brought their philosophy of working hard and seizing opportunity. Hundreds of thousands more arrived in the 1930s when Japan invaded China. By the eve of World War II, the population was more than one and a half million.

Government House and later constructions

A few hours after Japan's attack on the American fleet at Pearl Harbour in December 1941, a dozen Japanese battalions began an assault on Hong Kong; Hong Kong's minimal air force was destroyed on the airfield at Kai Tak within five minutes. Abandoning the New Territories and Kowloon, the defenders retreated to Hong Kong island, hoping for relief which never came. They finally surrendered on Christmas Day in 1941. Survivors recall three and a half years of hunger and hardship under the occupation forces, who deported many Hong Kong Chinese to the mainland.

A number of Hong Kong's monuments were damaged during this time: St John's Cathedral was turned into a military club, the old governor's lodge on the Peak was burned down, and the commandant of the occupation forces rebuilt the colonial governor's mansion in Japanese style.

At the end of World War II, Hong Kong took stock of what remained – the population was down to half a million, and there was no industry, no fishing fleet, and few houses and public services.

Hong Kong Makes a Comeback

China's civil war sent distressing echoes to Hong Kong. While the Chinese Communist armies drove towards the south, the flow of refugees into Hong Kong gathered force, and by the time the People's Republic of China was proclaimed in 1949, the total population of Hong Kong had grown to more than two million people. The fall of Shanghai in 1950 brought another flood of refugees, among them

Housing for the masses

many wealthy people and skilled artisans, including the Shanghai industrialists who became the founders of Hong Kong's now famous textile industry. In the late 1970s Hong Kong became the conduit for China's goods, investment, and tourism. It also found itself famous as a worldwide bargain shopping centre.

Housing was now in desperately short supply. Housing had always been scarce for Hong Kong's Chinese. The problem became an outright disaster on Christmas Day in 1953. An uncontrollable fire devoured a whole city of squatters' shacks in Kowloon; 50,000 refugees were deprived of shelter.

The calamity spurred the government to launch an emergency programme of public-housing construction; spartan new blocks of flats put cheap and fireproof roofs over hundreds of thousands of heads. But this new housing was grimly overcrowded, and even a frenzy of construction couldn't keep pace with the increasing demand for living space. In 1962 the colonial authorities closed the border with China, but even this did not altogether stem the flow of refugees: the next arrivals were the Vietnamese boat people.

Back to China

As 1997 drew nearer, it became clear that the Chinese government had no intention of renewing the 99-year lease on the New Territories. Negotiations began, and in 1984, Prime Minister Margaret Thatcher signed the Sino-British Joint Declaration, in which Britain confirmed the transfer of the New Territories and all of Hong Kong to China in 1997. For its part, China declared Hong Kong a 'Special Administrative Region' and guaranteed its civil and social system for at least 50 years after 1997.

Although China's Basic Law promised that Hong Kong's existing laws and civil liberties would be upheld, refugees began flowing the other way. The British Nationality Act (1981) had in effect prevented Hong Kong citizens from acquiring British citizenship, and thousands of people, anxious about their future under China's rule, were prompted to apply for citizenship elsewhere, notably in Canada and Australia. The protests in 1989 in Beijing's Tiananmen Square sparked sympathy marches in Hong Kong, and further increased tension with China. Some companies moved their headquarters out of Hong Kong.

Ironically, as the handover approached, the British granted the Hong Kong Chinese more political autonomy than they had done since the colony was founded, including such democratic reforms as elections to the Legislative Council.

Fresh Challenges

Since the handover in 1997, China has largely followed a hands-off policy, but critics say that since Tung Chee Hwa, Hong Kong's Chief Executive, is closely allied with Beijing, there is little reason for the mainland to intervene. Controversial internal security legislation, planned for 2003 but put on hold after large-scale public protests, is widely believed to be at Beijing's insistence.

Hong Kong's destiny has always been linked to the water

The Asian financial crisis of 1997 and world market slumps in the early 21st century scorched Hong Kong's economy, a beating from which it has yet to recover. And as another kick in the teeth, the territory was hit hard by the outbreak of Severe Acute Respiratory Syndrome (SARS) in 2003.

Historical Landmarks

7th–9th centuries AD Probable arrival of the Tanka People. Chinese fortress constructed in Tuen Mun.
10th–14th centuries Arrival of the 'Five Great Clans' in what is now the New Territories.
Early 16th century Portuguese traders reach Canton.
1557 Portugal establishes official trading colony at Macau.
1699 British East India Company establishes itself in Canton.
1840 First Opium War sparked by a Chinese imposed ban on the opium trade operated by British and American traders.
1841 British fleet attacks Canton and takes possession of Hong Kong.
1842 Under the Treaty of Nanking, China cedes Hong Kong to the British 'in perpetuity'.
1856–60 The British embark on the Second Opium War and force the opening of further ports and the cession of the Kowloon Peninsula.
1898 Britain negotiates a 99-year lease of the New Territories and the 233 Outlying Islands, until 30 June 1997.
1911 Qing dynasty falls; Sun Yat-sen forms the Republic of China.
1928 Mao Zedong establishes his first guerrilla base; in 1935 he takes control of the Chinese Communist Party.
1941 Hong Kong surrenders to the invading Japanese.
1945 Hong Kong returns to being a British colony.
1950–53 Communist victory on mainland China sees massive waves of refugees swell the local population. Industrialisation commences.
1966–69 Cultural Revolution brings unrest to Hong Kong, but the colony remains intact as China's secret trade outlet.
1978 Economic reforms after the death of Mao Zedong foster increased economic links with China.
1984 Margaret Thatcher and Chinese premier Zhao Ziyang sign the Joint Declaration for the return of the entire Hong Kong territory to China.
1997 China resumes sovereignty of Hong Kong.
2003 Hong Kong's economic woes compounded by the arrival of the SARS virus. Proposed internal security legislation provokes large-scale protests.

NEC
GOLDEN STAR

WHERE TO GO

The crowded Kowloon peninsula and the booming New Territories on the mainland call for some serious sightseeing; but we begin across Victoria Harbour on Hong Kong Island, where the city was first founded and which remains the centre of government, business and commerce.

HONG KONG ISLAND

Central District

No matter how many tunnels and transit systems speed up cross-harbour traffic, nothing matches the ride on the **Star Ferry** from Kowloon to **Central District** on Hong Kong Island across Victoria Harbour. As the green-and-white double-decker boats get ready to leave the pier, bells ring, the gangplank is raised and deck-hands man the hawsers. On the 7-minute crossing the ferry weaves its way through an obstacle course of both large and small craft, and the soaring skyline of Hong Kong Island draws nearer.

There are 12 boats in the Star Ferry fleet, all with star names: Morning Star, Northern Star, Golden Star, Meridian Star, Solar Star, Night Star, World Star, Shining Star, Twinkling Star, Day Star, Silver Star and Celestial Star. Which one did you take?

The waterfront on Hong Kong side used to continue further west of Central's Star Ferry Pier. But massive reclamation here has created space for the Airport Express terminus, **Hong Kong Station** and the **International Finance Centre** development. As you get off the ferry, the 52-storey **Jardine**

The Star Ferry crossing Victoria Harbour

House with porthole-shaped windows catches the eye. There are restaurants in the basement and you can access the raised pedestrian walkway from the escalators on the ground floor. Next to the Jardine building is **Exchange Square**, a complex with a large shopping mall; just behind it is the **General Post Office** with a philatelic centre on the ground floor.

On Connaught Road Central, you'll find one of Hong Kong's curiosities, the 800-m (2,625-ft) long outdoor

Feng Shui: Seeking Prosperity

Feng shui (or fung shui in Cantonese) literally means 'wind and water'. An ancient system of divination, its purpose is to achieve harmony with the forces of nature and produce an environment conducive to health and prosperity. Arranging physical premises according to the principles of *feng shui* deflects evil forces and assures the welfare of the inhabitants. Anyone moving into a new apartment will call in a *feng shui* geomancer to determine the optimum position of walls, doors and even furniture.

Buildings should face quiet water if possible, or have water nearby, such as a fish tank or a fountain. Lions and dragons are protective. The Hong Kong Bank's doors are guarded by a pair of bronze lions, and the China Resources Building by its Nine Dragons Wall. The famous Bank of China Tower, on the other hand, ignored *feng shui* principles, and is considered an untamed 'dragon's den'.

The dragons of Hong Kong must also receive consideration. New buildings must not block their accustomed pathways to the water, and in one case a new apartment block was constructed with a huge opening in its middle to allow the dragon's passage to the sea.

The Hong Kong Chinese are firmly committed to *feng shui*, and its principles are becoming popular in Europe and America. Inside China, however, visitors will find that such traditions are played down, perhaps in deference to what is considered a more 'modern' attitude.

Central Mid-Levels Escalator. It ferries commuters from the Mid-Levels apartment complexes downhill from 6 to 10am, and uphill from 10.20am to midnight. Nearby is **Central Market**, the wholesale food market of Hong Kong. To stroll around the ground floor meat stalls or teeming second-storey vegetable stands, be sure to arrive before noon, when activities wind down for the day and the vendors head off to lunch.

Modern design and bad *feng shui:* the Bank of China Tower

Just east of the Star Ferry terminal, you'll come to **City Hall**. No longer a centre of government, it now functions as a cultural centre. Go through the underground walkway to **Statue Square**; on the east side of the square is the **Legislative Council Building**, one of the few colonial buildings left in Hong Kong. So great is the pressure on the available land that most of Hong Kong's colonial architectural heritage has been demolished and replaced by new skyscrapers.

Nearby is **Chater Garden** and a number of notable architectural landmarks. Most famous is the striking 70-storey I.M. Pei-designed **Bank of China Tower**, not beloved by the people of Hong Kong – its triangular prisms and sharp angles violate the principles of *feng shui* *(see opposite)* and its radio masts stick up like an insect's antennae. The rival **Hong Kong Bank** is by architect Norman Foster; built on a 'coathanger frame', its floors hang rather than ascend. From inside the vast atrium you can view the whole structure as well as the mechanical workings of the building. Two bronze lions, carrying out *feng shui* principles, guard its doors.

You can catch one of Hong Kong's historic **trams** along Des Voeux Road and ride from Central to Causeway Bay *(see box, page 33)*. In 1904, the narrow, double-decker trams ran along the waterfront, but land reclamation has placed them far inland.

From the Bank of China Tower, make a short detour up Garden Road and turn into Battery Path to reach **St. John's Cathedral**. Built 1847–49, this Anglican foundation is Hong Kong's oldest church and is thought to be the oldest Anglican church in East Asia. Built in a mixture of neo-Gothic and Norman styles, during World War II the church was turned into a club for Japanese officers; it was restored after the war. Note the stained glass windows in the Quiet Chapel, designed by Joseph Edward Nuttgens in the late 1950s. Behind the church is the 1917 **French Mission Building**, now used as the Court of Final Appeal.

Across from the Bank of China Tower a winding path leads up to **Hong Kong Park**. The park's 10.5 hectares (25 acres) of landscaped gardens and lakes contains a large **greenhouse** that holds many species of plants, and an **aviary** of exotic birds.

In the park is **Flagstaff House**, Hong Kong's oldest colonial building, dating back to 1846. The two-storey whitewashed house now houses the **Museum of Tea Ware** (open Wed–Mon 10am–5pm; free), with exhibits describing the history of tea from the Warring

Inside St John's Cathedral

Flagstaff House, containing the Museum of Tea Ware

States period (475–221BC) to the present. Adjacent to the park is one of Hong Kong's largest and most up-market shopping malls, **Pacific Place**. Inside, it is packed with department stores, food halls, restaurants, art galleries, antiques shops and fashion boutiques.

Victoria Peak

For more than a century, the most exhilarating way up **Victoria Peak** (552m/1,713ft) has been by funicular. The **Peak Tram** starts its scenic climb just across the street and around the corner from the American Consulate in Garden Road and makes its way, sometimes at a startlingly steep incline, to the upper terminus at 398m (1,305ft). The right-of-way travels past fancy apartment blocks, bamboo stands and jungle flowers. Passengers crane their necks for dizzying glimpses of the harbour. The Peak is still the most fashionable place to live in Hong Kong, but real estate prices here are astronomi-

The Peak Galleria and Peak Tower offer restaurants, shopping, entertainment and spectacular views

cal; rents often reach around HK$50,000 a month. The Peak Tram, originally steam-powered, was built to speed the wealthy *taipans* to their mountainside retreats. Before the tram was built, sedan chairs and rickshaws were the only way to get here. Since the tram's inauguration in 1888 it has stopped only for typhoons and World War II.

The modern 120-passenger cars make the journey in around eight minutes. However, on sunny Saturdays and Sundays you may have to brave a crowd queuing up at the lower terminal. During the spring and autumn festivals, when people traditionally seek out the hilltops, the throngs are so large you would be better advised to try another time.

At the upper terminus there is a four-level shopping centre, the **Peak Galleria**. The neighbouring **Peak Tower**, which resembles an airport control tower, has a number of amusements, including the **Ripley's Believe It or Not!**

Odditorium (open Mon–Fri noon–8pm, Sat–Sun 11am–9pm; admission fee), complete with a real shrunken human head and headless hen, and **Madame Tussaud's** (open daily 11am–8pm; admission fee), with more than 100 lifelike wax portraits of celebrities. It is also possible to take themed virtual reality rides at the **Peak Explorer Motion Simulator**.

You can walk around the peak on Lugard and Harlech roads for impressive views of Hong Kong, the coastline and the islands in 45 minutes. The view is especially stunning at night. There are also souvenir stands, benches for a rest and some of Hong Kong's last surviving rickshaws – however these are not for rides, but are a tourist photo opportunity. If you're up to a climb, take the Mount Austin road to the **Victoria Peak Gardens**. These gardens used to belong to the governor's mountain lodge, but the building was demolished by the Japanese during the occupation of Hong Kong.

From the lower terminal of the Peak Tram it's only a short walk to the former governor's residence, **Government House** (since 1997 only used for special functions by Hong Kong's ruling body, and only open to the public a few times a year). Across from the mansion, the **Zoological and Botanical Gardens** (gardens open daily 6am–10pm; zoo 6am–7pm; free) provide a welcome oasis. In the very early morning the park is taken over by people doing *tai-chi* exercises. Both young and old go through ballet-like movements in slow motion to discipline the mind and body. The park's zoo has an interesting collection of jungle birds.

The Botanical Gardens

Western District

The Western District is one of Hong Kong's oldest neighbourhoods and its narrow streets hold a collection of fascinating traditional shops and enterprises. Opposite the Macau Ferry Terminal you'll find the **Western Market** (open 10am–7pm). It is more interesting for its architecture than for its shopping; it's situated in a four-storey Edwardian building built in 1906. For an interesting glimpse of small and family-owned shops, walk along Bonham Strand East and West, Man Wa Lane and Cleverly Street. You'll find herb and medicine shops, incense shops, chop makers' shops (makers of Chinese seals) and more.

Hong Kong University's campus is spread along Bonham Road. When it opened in 1912, the university had a total of 72 students; now it has around 14,000. At the top of a sloping driveway is the original Edwardian university building, now presiding over the institution's more recent structures. The University's **Fung Ping Shan Museum**, 94 Bonham Road (open Mon–Sat 9.30am–6pm, Sun 1.30–5.30pm; free) holds a significant collection of antiquities: bronzes dating from 3000BC and ceramics, including Han Dynasty tomb pottery. It also has the world's largest collection of Nestorian crosses from the Yuan Dynasty period.

Chop maker at work

Take the Central Mid-Levels Escalator to **Hollywood Road**, known for its antiques and curio shopping. Here the windows and open doors of the shops reveal an alluring selection of Asian furniture, carpets, carvings, porcelain and bronze.

Walk west along Hollywood Road until you come to **Man Mo Temple**, the island's oldest house of worship (though the date of its founding is subject to dispute). Visitors entering the temple are confronted by a dense pall of smoke from all the burning joss sticks and the incense coils hanging from the ceiling (these will burn for as long as a month). The gold-plated sedan chairs on the left-hand side of the temple were once used for transporting the statues of the temple's gods in religious processions. The statues in the main shrine represent Man, the god of literature, and Mo, the god of war, a curious juxtaposition. The temple is always crowded with worshippers.

Incense coils hang from the ceiling at the Man Mo Temple

Just past the temple is the aptly named Ladder Street. Go down one flight of steps to Upper Lascar Row, popularly known as **Cat Street**, for more antiques and curio shops. The nickname apparently refers to the cat burglars who once sold their stolen goods here.

Walk up the steps to reach Caine Lane, where you'll find the **Museum of Medical Sciences** (open Tues–Sat 10am–5pm, Sun 1–5pm; admission fee). The interesting Edwardian building was formerly the Pathological Institute, founded to combat the 19th century's 30-year-long

Trams trundling along Des Voeux Road

outbreak of bubonic plague. The old laboratory is still intact and there are interesting exhibits on the historical development of medical sciences in Hong Kong and on the interface between Chinese and Western medicine.

Wan Chai

Situated just to the east of the financial district, Wan Chai was once an area of sleazy clubs and topless bars; this was the setting for *The World of Suzy Wong*. Servicemen relaxing from the rigours of the Vietnam War poured millions of dollars into the Wan Chai boom of the 1960s. There's still a rash of tacky girly clubs here, but also plenty of regular pubs and a smattering of smart cocktail and theme bars.

The Wan Chai waterfront is dominated by the **Hong Kong Convention and Exhibition Centre**, the largest in Asia, which includes hotels, theatres and exhibition halls. The convention centre, an extension on reclaimed land, affords stunning views of the Wan Chai waterfront. Behind is **Central Plaza**, Hong Kong's tallest building and the world's eighth highest, at 374m (1,227ft). Just west of the convention centre is another modern highlight, the **Hong Kong Academy for Performing Arts** on Gloucester Road. Opposite is the black-bricked **Hong Kong Arts Centre**, a thriving hub for the arts scene in the city with its theatres, cinema and art galleries.

On Wan Chai's Bowen Road, **Maiden's Rock**, also called Lover's Rock, is the gathering place for the annual Maiden's festival. The rock is steeped in tradition. Every August young women convene to light joss sticks and some even climb the 9-m (30-ft) rock to pray for good husbands.

Causeway Bay and Beyond

About 2km (a mile) east of Wan Chai, **Causeway Bay** is second only to Tsim Sha Tsui as Hong Kong's place to shop. A prosperous tourist district, it is full of shopping centres and department stores, along with a number of good restaurants. The busy night-and-day crowds make this area vibrant and lively.

On the nautical side is the **Causeway Bay Typhoon Shelter**, where expensive yachts are moored, and the Hong Kong Yacht Club has its headquarters. Across Gloucester Road,

Take a Tram

The ancient tram system that travels along Des Voeux, Hennessy and Causeway roads is the most leisurely and revealing way to see Hong Kong. With more than 32km (20 miles) of track, the jerky electric double-deckers cover almost the entire north coast of the island. Enter at the back of the tram, and try to get a seat in the front of the upper deck for the best views of Hong Kong's colourful streets, always crowded with shoppers and nonstop day-and-night activity. You'll pass through Wan Chai, where the world of Suzy Wong once existed, and travel all the way to the eastern extremity of Shau Kei Wan, once a pirates' hangout, and still with a colony of 'boat people' who live on junks and sampans moored in the bay.

The western terminus is in Kennedy Town, an overcrowded section of the city, named after a 19th-century Hong Kong governor, Sir Arthur Kennedy. When you're ready to get off the tram, just drop your HK$2 fare in the box at the front beside the driver.

opposite the World Trade Centre, is the **Noon Day Gun**, which under British rule was sounded on the stroke of midday. Silent for a time, the tradition has been revived and is a tourist attraction.

It's not clear how the custom started. One story has it that traders Jardine, Matheson & Co fired a private salute for a visiting tycoon, an act that incensed the colonial authorities, who felt that they had the sole right to issue such a 21-gun welcome. As a result, the merchants were forced to limit their salvoes to one a day – and from then on, they signalled the noon hour daily for all to hear. The gun was made famous by Noel Coward's satirical song, *Mad Dogs and Englishmen.*

Farther east is Hong Kong's largest park, **Victoria Park**, with sports grounds and other facilities. On the eastern side of

Typhoon Alert

No natural danger poses more of a threat to Hong Kong than a typhoon (*dai fung* or 'big wind' in Cantonese). Typhoons always cause damage, and disastrous typhoons have occurred over and over throughout Hong Kong's history. Despite modern techniques of surveillance and early warning, there are casualties and damage almost every year. Typhoons generally occur between July and September.

A series of signals from one to ten alerts residents in the event of a storm. Signal No. 1 goes up when a tropical storm that could escalate into a typhoon has moved within a 740-km (460-mile) radius of Hong Kong. People generally pay little attention at this point. Signal 3 means that the winds have escalated, accompanied, perhaps, by heavy rains. Tours and harbour cruises are suspended, and some businesses close.

No. 8 is more serious: it means that the gale has reached Hong Kong. Banks, offices, museums and most shops and restaurants close, and all transport is suspended. In case of a No. 8 warning, you should remain in your hotel and check the storm's progress on TV or radio.

Victoria Park on Causeway Road is **Tin Hau Temple**, dedicated to Tin Hau, the Taoist Queen of Heaven and patroness of seafarers. Originally the temple was on the shore, but reclamation projects have now left it high and dry. On the 23rd day of the Third Moon, the birthday of the goddess is celebrated here and in all Hong Kong fishing communities.

A night at the races at Happy Valley

At the eastern end of Hong Kong Island, past North Point and Quarry Bay, and best reached on foot (15 minutes) from Shau Kei Wan MTR station, is the **Kong Kong Museum of Coastal Defence** (open Fri–Wed 10am–5pm; admission fee). Housed in the restored Lei Yue Mun Fort, which was built by the British, it showcases 600 years of coastal defence in southern China, from the Mong dynasty to the 1997 handover. Included are informative videos and displays on the Opium Wars and the Japanese invasion of Hong Kong in 1941.

Happy Valley

Inland from the bay is **Happy Valley**. At one time this was a very miserable valley, a swampland conducive only to breeding malarial mosquitoes. It is now home to Hong Kong's first racecourse. Hong Kong's gamblers are so eager to play the horses that, despite the opening of a bigger and better racecourse at Sha Tin, the **Happy Valley Racecourse** is thriving.

Be sure to visit the **Hong Kong Racing Museum** (open Tues–Sun 10am–5pm; race days 10am–12.30pm; free), which traces the history of the sport.

Aberdeen harbour

Aberdeen

Aberdeen is the island's oldest settlement. Once a pirate lair, it is home to the 'floating population' – the 'boat people' who spend their entire lives on the junks in the harbour, some proudly claiming never to have set foot on land (except for funerals, which don't count). The majority of the 'boat people' have moved to nearby highrises but a sizeable seaborne community remains. The junks are a picturesque sight: children frolicking on the poop deck, women preparing food or playing mahjong, elderly folk watching the sunset, dogs and cats underfoot, songbirds in bamboo cages overhead – and all afloat. The boats may appear deceptively primitive, but many of them have their own electric generators and all the conveniences of modern housing. There are fewer boats now than in the past; many boat people, especially the younger generation, now live on dry land. You can take a tour of the port in one of the small *sampan*. A half-hour tour costs HK$50; pay at the end, or the driver may cut short your trip.

Aberdeen's theatrical **Jumbo Floating Restaurant** has been a tourist attraction for many years. The food may not live up to expectations, but the fantasy environment makes up for it. If you can get up early enough, you can attend the pre-dawn auction held at the vast local wholesale **fish market**; otherwise, have a look at the street market that is held later in the day.

Ocean Park

The peninsula opposite the east coast of Ap Lei Chau island is home to **Ocean Park** (open daily 10am–6pm; admission HK$180 adults, HK$90 children 11 years and under), one of Hong Kong's biggest attractions. It is divided into three areas: a highland, a lowland and the Middle Kingdom. Linking the lowland and highland sections of the park, a cable-car system offers spectacular views across to the islands of the South China Sea.

Until Disney Land opens its doors on Lantau Island sometime in 2005, Ocean Park is the territory's sole amusement park of any stature. There's an enormous oceanarium with dolphins, seal lions, seals, penguins and sharks, a pair of bamboo-munching pandas – An An and Jia Jia, an amazing recreation of an atoll reef with flying rays and layers and layers of sea life, and a host of stomach-wrenching rides – the latest edition is the freefall Abyss Turbo Drop.

Cable cars at Ocean Park

Repulse Bay

Continuing around the coast in a counter-clockwise direction, Deep Water Bay offers a good beach and harbours. The next inlet is **Repulse Bay**, a roomy, sandy crescent backed by green hills and always busy with daytrippers and sunbathers. Notice the massive wall of condominiums, built in the 1980s. The story has it that the developers left the space in the middle of the curving facade for good *feng shui* – to enable the mountain's 'dragon spirit' to retain access to the sea.

Stanley

Stanley was once one of the main fishing villages on Hong Kong Island. The well-known **Stanley Market** (10am–6pm) is a major source for bargain clothing and other merchandise. The waterfront is lined with fine restaurants and bars, many of them with balconies offering sea views. A few minutes by foot along the coast past the Tin Hau temple and opposite Stanley Plaza is Murray House – a former British Army building that stood in Central until 1982, when its stones were carefully dismantled, numbered and then rebuilt in Stanley. Inside are more shops and restaurants.

***Feng shui* principles brought to bear in Repulse Bay**

Shek O

Further along the coast, on the eastern side of the island, is Shek O, a seaside village with narrow winding streets, a decent beach and some good restaurants. There are great walks into the surrounding hills, and the beach gets packed out on sunny weekends with local families enjoying BBQs.

The Hong Kong Cultural Centre in Kowloon is the city's unofficial headquarters for the performing arts

KOWLOON

Though much smaller than Hong Kong Island, Kowloon has almost twice the population. In many areas, the density reaches the equivalent of 150,000 inhabitants per square kilometre (a quarter of a square mile).

Most of Kowloon's attractions for visitors are centered near the tip of the peninsula in the district known as **Tsim Sha Tsui**. Adjacent to the Star Ferry terminal is **Ocean Terminal**, where international cruise ships dock, and the gigantic **Harbour City**, a modern complex of malls, hotels and restaurants.

Waterfront

If you walk east on the Star Ferry terminal concourse, you will find yourself on the wonderful **Waterfront Promenade**, which begins at the **Clock Tower**, all that

A stroll along the Waterfront Promenade should be done at least twice during any stay in Hong Kong, once by day and once by night. And if you're in Hong Kong for Chinese New Year, this is the place to be to see the fireworks bursting across the city.

remains of the once grand Kowloon-Canton Railway Terminus, which was pulled down in 1975 and replaced by a modern building in Hung Hom. Don't rely on the clock tower times: the four clocks on the faces of the tower are not synchronised and therefore do not always show the same time.

The promenade offers unparalled views of the harbour and Hong Kong Island. If you continue to the end of the promenade, you will be in Tsim Sha Tsui East, a busy commercial district built on more than 60 hectares (150 acres) of reclaimed land.

Flanked by the clock tower is the imposing **Hong Kong Cultural Centre**. Hong Kong's major venue for the performing arts, the building has been criticised for its fortress-like architecture and windowless façade on a site which enjoys one of the most magnificent views in the world. The interior is a comfortable amalgam of Chinese and Western design, with an impressive main lobby. The centre contains two large concert halls, frequently used by the Hong Kong Philharmonic Orchestra, and a studio theatre, plus a library, an exhibition gallery, shops, restaurants and bars.

Museums

Next door is the **Hong Kong Space Museum** (open Mon, Wed–Fri 1–9pm; Sat and Sun 10am–9pm; closed Tues; admission fee; separate admission to theatre). Its futuristic dome design is striking; inside are interactive exhibits, including one in which you can experience weightlessness. The theatre presents 'sky shows' and IMAX films.

The **Hong Kong Museum of Art** (open Fri–Wed, 10am–6pm; admission fee) stands behind the Space Museum next to the cultural centre. It contains the Xubaizhi collection of painting and calligraphy; galleries devoted to antiquities and ceramics; and a gallery of work by artists who belong to the contemporary Hong Kong School. Also of interest is the collection of paintings and photographs of old Hong Kong. The museum mounts special exhibitions and has an excellent gift shop.

A few blocks up Chatham Road South are two more major museums. The **Hong Kong Science Museum** (open Mon–Wed and Fri 1–9pm, Sat and Sun 10am–9pm, closed Thur; admission fee) is a state-of-the-art interactive museum that will teach you how everything and anything works from ancient sailing ships to the latest technology.

The **Hong Kong Museum of History** (open Mon and Wed–Sat 10am–6pm, Sun 10am–7pm, closed Tues; admission fee) opened its new permanent exhibition *The Hong Kong Story* in 2001, with spectacular interactive exhibits showcasing 6,000 years of Hong Kong's history and cultural heritage.

The Hong Kong Museum of Art

Peninsula Hotel

Just across Salisbury Road from the cultural centre is the historic **Peninsula**

Hotel, now expanded and modernised by a 32-storey tower *(see page 132)*. Opened in 1928, the Peninsula was the first hotel on Kowloon, strategically positioned for passengers travelling overland to Europe by train. The lobby became the favourite rendezvous for high society, and to this day, guests sit beneath the restored gilt stucco ceiling to see and be seen. Afternoon high tea or evening cocktails to strains of the resident string orchestra are a wonderful way for visitors to recapture the atmosphere of a bygone age, but do pay attention to your attire.

Nathan Road

Alongside the hotel runs busy **Nathan Road**, Hong Kong's fabled shopping street, lined with shops, hotels and restaurants. Kowloon's main street was created by Sir Matthew Nathan when he was governor of Hong Kong at the turn of

The lights of Kowloon's Nathan Road

the 19th century. When it was constructed, many thought it absurd to have a tree-lined boulevard running through what was practically wilderness. Now the former 'Nathan's Folly' is known as the 'Golden Mile'.

The mosque on the south-east corner of Kowloon Park is the territory's largest with three storeys and four minarets. Hong Kong has around 80,000 Muslims.

A few blocks up Nathan Road is **Kowloon Park** (open daily 6am–midnight), elegantly laid out with fountains, promenades and ornamental gardens; be sure to go up the steps to see the Sculpture Walk, where artists from Hong Kong and other countries exhibit their works of art. Further up Nathan Street is **Yau Ma Tei**, one of the older parts of Kowloon. Turn off Nathan and walk down Kansu Street to find the **Jade Market** (open 9am–6pm), with more than 100 stalls spread out in a large tent, just before you reach the overpass.

Temple Street Night Market

Hong Kong's liveliest market scene is the **Temple Street Night Market** (open 4pm–midnight), near Jordan Road. Everything is sold here, from clothing to souvenirs to electronic goods, and bargaining is an intrinsic part of the shopping experience. The market is known for its pavement food stalls, where you can dine inexpensively on seafood.

The market runs all the way up to **Tin Hau Temple**, where you will find fortune tellers' tables (some speak English) and possibly street performers singing Chinese opera (or pop songs). The temple is one of many in Hong Kong dedicated to Tin Hau, goddess of seafarers; this one also houses an altar to Shing Wong, the city's god. In the daytime the temple (open 8am–6pm) attracts worshippers, while its park attracts strollers and mahjong players.

Yuen Po Street Bird Garden

Nathan Road goes all the way up to **Boundary Street**, which marks the boundary between Kowloon and the New Territories. Near Boundary Street, off Prince Edward Street West, is the **Yuen Po Street Bird Garden** (open 8am–7pm). Songbirds are popular pets in Chinese households; their owners take them for walks every day, carrying the cages through the streets. Here, the birds entertain passers-by with a symphony of shrill arias; as well as birds, you will find intricately-made cages for sale.

Further north in Sham Shui Po, west of the junction of Nathan Road and Boundary Street, is the **Lei Cheng Uk Han Tomb and Museum** on Tonkin Road (open Mon–Wed and Fri–Sat 10am–6pm, Sun 1–6pm; closed Thur). This ancient burial vault is believed to date back to the Han Dynasty (AD25–220). The barrel-vaulted chambers were discovered during excavations for a nearby housing development.

Wong Tai Sin

One of Hong Kong's brightest, biggest and busiest temples is ➤ the Sik Sik Yuen **Wong Tai Sin Temple** in central Kowloon. It is dedicated to a shepherd boy from Zhejiang who had special healing powers and came to be revered as a demi-god after his death. The incense-wreathed temple complex, which has halls dedicated to the Taoist, Confucian and Buddhist faiths, is especially packed out at Lunar New Year with locals praying for prosperity and rattling fortune sticks.

Locals at Wong Tai Sin

A picturesque bay on the Sai Kung peninsula

NEW TERRITORIES

Hong Kong's New Territories begin at Boundary Street in Price Edward. Surprises spring up on all sides: new industrial complexes alongside sleepy farming villages, skyscraper towns in the middle of nowhere, Hakka women in their traditional flat straw hats with hanging black trim, water buffalo and flashes of azalea everywhere.

The New Territories can be explored by taking the **Kowloon–Canton Railway** (KCR), which makes 10 stops between the station in Kowloon and Sheung Shui, the last stop before entering China. Ask the tourist authority about its interesting **Heritage Tour** from Kowloon and other countryside tours *(see page 113)*.

Tsuen Wan

The main highway makes a circuit of the New Territories, beginning with the new town of **Tsuen Wan**, situated in an area of heavy industry just west of Kowloon. Set amid Tsuen Wan's residential towers, a short walk from the MTR station, is the 18th-century walled village of **Sam Tung Uk**. Built by a Chan clan in 1786, it is now preserved as a museum (open Wed–Mon, 9am–5pm). On display is period furniture and farming implements, as well as exhibitions on Chinese folk culture.

North of the town, a commanding view over the New Territories to the north can be seen from **Tai Mo Shan**, Hong Kong's highest peak at 957m (3,140ft). The highway continues parallel to the coast. One-third of all Hong Kong's beaches are to be found in a single 14-km (9-mile) stretch of this region's shoreline. Place names are often based on the distance to the nearest mile-post, as measured from the tip of the Kowloon peninsula. Thus you will find '19½ mile Beach' at Castle Peak Bay.

Window on China

The main road continues clockwise around the New Territories. As you approach the border, you can see the skyscrapers of **Shenzhen**, one of China's most successful Special Economic Zones, but whose main attraction for tourists is its cheap shopping *(see page 75)*. The lookout point at Lok Ma Chau was once known as Hong Kong's 'window on China'. In the years of China's isolation from the West, tourists would come to the lookout point here to get a glimpse of the great mystery beyond.

A slower pace of life after the bustle of Hong Kong

Temple courtyard at Ching Chung Koon

Tuen Mun

Not far away, at milepost 21 near the large new town of Tuen Mun, is a Taoist retreat known as **Ching Chung Koon**. This 'Temple of Green Pines' is a spacious complex containing temples and pavilions, statues and gardens. It is known for its collection of bonsai and houses a jade seal more than 1,000 years old. Among the ponds is one inhabited by turtles: visitors toss in coins in the hope of bouncing one off a turtle's head as a way of achieving good fortune.

Walled Villages

An even more interesting image from Chinese history is the walled village of **Kat Hing Wai**, in the village of Kam Tin just outside the market town of Yuen Long. This is the most easily accessible of the New Territories' walled villages. The village is built in a square, and the only way in is through the gate in the brick defensive wall. Kat Hing Wai was built

Tang chung Ling Ancestral Hall

four or five centuries ago by the Hakka Tang clan, one of the Five Great Clans that migrated here from North China *(see page 11)*. Many of the old houses in the village have been replaced by modern structures.

The Tang clan's earliest walled village was **Lo Wai**, which also has its defensive wall intact. Adjacent to the village is the restored **Tang Chung Ling Ancestral Hall** (open Wed–Mon 9am–1pm and 2–5pm), which dates from the early 16th century. Few traditional ancestral halls remain in China since the anti-historical destruction during the Cultural Revolution, so these New Territories ancestral halls are rare survivors. Another such hall, belonging to the Liu Clan, is Liu Man Shek Tong in the village of Sheung Shui.

Tai Fu Tai

➤ One of the most interesting sites in the New Territories is **Tai Fu Tai** (open Wed–Mon 9am–1pm and 2–5pm), another rare survivor, this one a mansion that belonged to a Confucian high official. The house was built in 1865 by a member of the Man clan who achieved the rank of *tai fu* (mandarin) by doing well in the Imperial Examinations. The preservation of this wonderful home is ongoing; a projected restoration of the original garden is still in progress. The traditional Qing Dynasty style of the mansion is enlivened by a few Western touches: a Baroque-style ceiling and stained glass above the doorways, showing the builder's modern attitude at the time of construction.

Tai Po

The highway and the railway stay close together from Fanling, site of the best golf courses in the area. **Tai Po**, just south of Fanling, is known for its market, **Tai Po Market**, which buzzes with activity daily from 7am to 6pm. Just up a lane from the market is the **Man Mo Temple**, with long-burning incense coils hanging from its ceiling, a popular spot dedicated to the Taoist gods of war and literature.

Sai Kung

The railway line then curves gracefully around Tolo Harbour, an idyllic body of water well-protected from the open sea. You can take a ferryboat (the pier is a 10-minute walk from University station) through the harbour, past the ingenious **Plover Cove** reservoir, a water catchment area appropriated by damming and draining a broad inlet from the sea. The boats go on to the friendly fishermen's island of **Tap Mun**, in Mirs Bay, with stops in remote hamlets of the **Sai Kung Peninsula**. The Sai Kung area is the location of two official parks and nature preserves, while on the south side

Make a Wish

If you need to change your luck, visit the Wishing Tree in the lush valley of Lam Tsuen, near Tai Po in the New Territories. There are actually two wishing trees; the desiccated one, struck by lightning, is purported to be the real wishing tree, but the one near the road, a large banyan, is prettier. In any case, from the nearby temple you can secure an orange tied to swatches of red paper. Write your wishes on the paper, and see how high you can throw your orange into the tree. The higher it goes, the more chance you have of your wish coming true. There's also a wishing tree in the Zu Miao temple if you visit Foshan near Guangzhou *(see page 74)*.

of the peninsula are some of the territory's best beaches. Also at University station, the modern campus of the **Chinese University of Hong Kong** is visible. Teaching here is conducted in both Chinese and English. The **Art Gallery** (open Mon–Sat 10am–4.45pm, Sun 2.30–5.30pm) in the Institute of Chinese Studies Building is worth a visit for its painting and calligraphy collections.

Sha Tin

➤ **Sha Tin** is the site of the **Man Fat Tze**, also known as the Monastery of 10,000 Buddhas, set on a hillside above the burgeoning town. There are hundreds of stone steps to walk up before you reach the monastery with its regiments of small gilt statues of Buddha (no less than 12,800 of them) lining the walls. The monastery was founded in 1957 by the monk Yuet Kai, who died in 1965 at the age of 87. He had previously predicted that his body would not decompose if he were to be buried behind the temple in a crouching position. True enough, when his disciples exhumed the body eight months later, they found it still in good condition. They covered his

Wild and Beautiful

Remote areas of the New Territories and sections of Lantau Island are happy sighting grounds for birdwatchers. Hundreds of species have been recorded, from everyday egrets and funny-faced cockatoos to mynahs and pelicans. The Sai Kung Peninsula Nature Preserve has many hiking trails for the nature lover.

As civilisation encroaches, wild animals have been vanishing: leopards have not been seen in 20 years. But you can still come across barking deer, monkeys, porcupines and scaly anteaters. In the wilderness you may also stumble upon a banded krait, a cobra, or some other fearsome snake. Though sightings are common, bitings are rare.

corpse in gold leaf and placed it in a building on the second level. Some indefatigable climbers will want to go up to the top of the nine-storey pink pagoda for a panoramic view.

The pagoda at Man Fat Tze, the Temple of 10,000 Buddhas

Also located in Sha Tin, by the Shing Mun River Channel, is the fabulous **Hong Kong Heritage Museum** (open Mon, Wed–Sat 10am–6pm, Sun 10am–7pm; admission fee). The museum contains a fun interactive guide to Cantonese opera, art galleries showing ancient and contemporary work from all over Asia as well as exhibits dedicated to telling the story of Hong Kong's culture and history.

Down to earth, the **Sha Tin Racecourse** can accommodate more than 80,000 spectators and is equipped with every imaginable luxury, including a giant video screen facing the stands, and for the horses, air-conditioned stables. Opposite the Sha Tin railway station, **New Town Plaza** features shops, cinemas and even a computer-controlled musical fountain.

Two natural rock formations are always pointed out on excursions. Sha Tin Rock, better known as **Amah (Mother) Rock**, is actually a pile of several rocks that resemble a woman with a baby in a sling on her back. Legend has it that a local woman climbed the hill every day to watch for her husband returning from across the sea; one day the wife and her child were turned to stone as a permanent symbol of her enduring faith. Closer to town is **Lion Rock**, shaped like a lion lying in wait.

A ferry arrives at Silvermine Bay, Lantau

OUTLYING ISLANDS

Excursion companies sell a variety of orientation cruises of Hong Kong harbour that include a look at some of its 235 outlying islands. These pleasant, but expensive, outings can lay the foundation for your own explorations aboard the cheap but usually comfortable ferries used by the islanders themselves. From the ferry terminals on Hong Kong Island you can escape to islands without cars or cares, where the local people smile 'hello' and, if you're lucky, point you to a secret beach for the ultimate in quality leisure time. For ferry information, *see page 120*.

You can buy an Island Hopping Pass for HK$30 from First Ferry Company, which allows you to jump on any ferry (except fast ferries) to Lantau, Cheung Chau and Peng Chau and back to Hong Kong in one day. Buy from the HKTB or ferry piers.

Lantau

The mountainous island of Lantau is the biggest in the colony, and covers nearly twice the area of Hong Kong Island. Ferries depart from Central every two hours between 6.10am and 10.30pm to **Silvermine Bay (Mui Wo)**, where a bus terminal has buses to all parts of the island. There are also ferries to Discovery Bay.

Lantau is no longer quite the island of tranquillity it once was. Since the completion of Hong Kong International Airport at Chek Lap Kok on the northwest coast, the population has increased considerably; a New Town has engulfed the sleepy coastal village of Tung Chung and construction is well underway for a Hong Kong Disneyland which opens in 2005. Yet much of the island remains rural, with more than half of it protected as parkland. There is a 69-km (43-mile) circular hiking trail *(see page 90)*. At 934m (3,064ft), **Lantau Peak** is high enough to attract the occasional rain cloud – refreshingly cool breezes blow on most hot summer days.

Visitors intending to include a beach interlude in their itinerary should head for **Cheung Sha Beach**, 3km (2 miles) long and popular for its beautiful white sand and excellent facilities.

The most famous site on the island is the world's tallest seated bronze statue of Buddha at 22m (73ft), the ➤ **Tiantan Buddha**. The statue and a small museum are perched on a peak, up 268 steps, above **Po Lin Monastery**, set in the glorious upland scenery of central Lantau. The monastery

The giant Tiantan Buddha at Po Lin Monastery

(open daily 10am–6pm; vegetarian lunch, noon–4pm) is strictly vegetarian and visitors are warned not to bring any meat with them. You can have a delicious vegetarian lunch here for a nominal cost.

From the monastery, hikers can enjoy the two-hour scenic cross-country trek down to Silvermine Bay, but be on the lookout for snakes, which can be plentiful in the Lantau hinterland, especially in summer. The hillsides that surround the monastery are the site of Hong Kong's only tea plantation. Visitors are welcome to visit the 24-hectare (60-acre) establishment and may sample the end product, Lantau tea.

During the 19th century, what is now the sleepy fishing village of **Tai O** was of great importance for the island, thanks to its location overlooking the Pearl River Estuary with its access to the city of Canton (Guangzhou), the most important trading and economic centre in South China. Today the people of this picturesque village make their living by fishing, duck-breeding and food-processing. Many of the inhabitants live – by choice, not necessarily through economic hardship – on the water, aboard houseboats or in houses on stilts in the main creek.

The creek at Tai O

A **Trappist monastery**, situated on a hillside overlooking the east coast of Lantau, is also open to visitors. To get here, follow the path from the southwest end of Discovery Bay; the walk takes about 30 minutes.

Cheung Chau

Some 10km (6 miles) west of Hong Kong lies the small, crowded island of **Cheung**

In the Harbour at Cheung Chau

Chau, only around one square mile in size. More than 25,000 people live here, many of them by fishing, but there is also an expat community, attracted by the laid-back Mediterranean ambience. The island has a checkered past of smuggling and piracy. That era is gone now, but other elements of the island's old life are preserved. The people still carve jade and build seaworthy junks, all by hand. Fish (heads discreetly wrapped in paper) are still hung out to dry in the sun.

Cheung Chau becomes the centre of Hong Kong life once a year, usually in May, during the **Bun Festival**, a folklore extravaganza *(see page 93)*. For the rest of the year, life goes on at its accustomed pace: rickety machines chugging in two-man factories, children in school uniforms being ferried home to houseboats and elderly fishermen stirring shrimp paste.

By way of formal tourist attractions, **Pak Tai Temple**, built in 1783, has some fine carvings and a great iron sword said to be 600 years old. Pak Tai is the Cantonese name for

Pak Tai temple on Cheung Chau

'Ruler of the North' and he is usually represented in a sitting position, with his feet resting on a tortoise and a snake. The statue of Pak Tai is credited with saving the village from a plague that broke out in Cheung Chau in the 18th century.

From the main township of **Cheung Chau** it's possible to take a walk via the harbour road (15 minutes) or the scenic Peak Road (45 minutes) to the village of **San Wai**, which has a temple dedicated to Tin Hau, goddess of the sea and protectress of fisherfolk. You can also take a *kai do*, or water taxi from the pier next to the ferry pier.

The **Praya**, the promenade in front of the ferry pier, is a good place to observe the many junks and fishing boats in the harbour. There are also several open-air restaurants where you can enjoy fresh seafood. At the other side of the island, at the end of Tung Wan Road, is **Tung Wan Beach**, the most popular beach on Cheung Chau. Further along the headland is Kwun Yam Wan beach, where you can rent boards from the windsurfing centre. San San, Hong Kong's gold medallist in windsurfing at the 1996 Olympics practised here.

Lamma

Less than 30 minutes by fast ferry from Central, sleepy Lamma Island is perfect for swimming, hiking, picnicking, birdwatching, or just relaxing. Hong Kong's third largest island has a population of only about 12,000; it is still largely undeveloped and has a laid-back atmosphere. Archaeologists indicate that Lamma has probably been inhabited for some 4,000 years and the island is known as 'Hong Kong's Stone Age Island'.

Try and plan a trip during a weekday, as Lamma tends to be swamped by daytrippers at the weekend. The principal settlements on the island are **Yung Shue Wan** on Lamma's northwest coast and **Sok Kwu Wan** on the east coast. Both villages offer good waterfront restaurants with homestyle Chinese food, principally seafood fresh from the tank. The ports are within hiking distance of several beautiful beaches and within a one-hour hike of each other on a marked trail. You can build up an appetite for dinner by making your way from the beach to the restaurant. Yung Shue Wan is still a very western expat residential enclave, with many boisterous pubs and Western-style restaurants.

Laid-back Lamma is a 35-minute ferry ride from Central

EXCURSION TO MACAU

Macau, the final bastion of Portugal's great 16th-century empire, is much more than just a quirk of history. Here, where East and West first met, life combines the spirit of Asia with something of the sunny atmosphere of the Mediterranean.

Macau's **historic centre**, the Largo do Senado, with its colonial architecture, has a distinctly Mediterranean flavour. Colonnaded public buildings, iron balconies, winding streets, flagstoned squares and the many churches all speak of the Portuguese inheritance as well as the Chinese, a fusion of East and West that has produced the unique Macanese culture.

The story of the European discovery of Macau begins in 1513 when Portuguese explorer Jorge Alvares reached the south coast of China. Traders followed in his wake, setting up bases in several parts of the Pearl River estuary. Finally, in 1557, they were all consolidated in Macau. It was the only European gateway to China, and through Macau flowed Western technology and religion. In 1576 Pope Gregory XIII created the Macau diocese, covering all of China and Japan.

No less impressive were the secular challenges. China and Japan were not on speaking terms, so trade between them had to be channelled through a neutral middleman. Lucky Macau was ideal for the job. Portugal's resulting near-monopoly of East–West trade understandably awakened the competitive instincts of other European powers. The Dutch sent an invasion flotilla to Macau in 1622, but the defenders triumphed. However, the end of the golden age was drawing near. China began to relax trade restrictions, and with the rise of Hong Kong, Macau became an isolated Portuguese outpost.

A haven for persecuted Japanese Christians in the 17th century, Portugal's neutrality during World War II assured

The remaining façade of the ruined St Paul's Church, Macau

the territory a flood of refugees. They were joined by a swarm of spies of all conceivable nationalities, and Macau won a name for international intrigue.

The territory was formally handed back to China in 1999. Now known as the Macau Special Administrative Region (MSAR), it is governed under a similar 'one country, two systems' set-up that Hong Kong enjoys. Over the past 10 years, its landscape has changed significantly with huge land reclamation projects creating artifical lakes, new highrise skyscrapers, a 338-m (1,109-ft) tower, casinos and a bridge connection to mainland China. But despite its plunge into the 21st century, a lot of Macau's colonial charm remains untouched.

Getting to and Around Macau

The easiest way to get to Macau is by jetfoil, operated by TurboJet (tel: 2859 3333). The 64-km (40-mile) trip takes about an hour. Departures are from the Macau Ferry Terminal in Sheung Wan just west of Central in the Shun Tak Centre. Jetfoils leave every 15 to 30 minutes 24 hours a day. The helpful Macau Government Tourist Office at 336–337 Shun Tak Centre (tel: 2857 2287) can assist with information. Entry procedures are similar to those in Hong Kong – most nationalities need only a passport to enter Macau. Macau's own currency, the *pataca*, is pegged to the Hong Kong dollar, and you can use your Hong Kong currency freely in Macau.

If you haven't picked up maps and brochures of Macau, be sure to visit the Macau Government Tourist Office at the Macau Ferry Terminal. Outside the terminal there are taxis as well as buses to all points (take 3, 3A, 10, or 10A to the historic centre; exact change is required). You'll also be approached by pedicab drivers; these are tricycles carrying two passengers. Pedicabs were once the most common form of transportation in Macau, but today they are mainly a tourist attraction.

Traditional Macau pedicab

Macau's population is about 440,000, a remarkably high figure for such a small area; land reclamation has eased the situation to some extent. If a trace of tropical lethargy still adds to the charm in this city of pavement cafés, palm trees and pedicabs, any torpor definitely ends once inside the doors of Macau's casinos, scene of some of the liveliest gambling west of Las Vegas. Gambling, a passion among both Hong Kong and mainland Chinese, provides almost 40 percent of the government's tax revenues and is a major source of employment.

Sights in Macau

If arriving from Hong Kong, the first casino you'll see in Macau is the vast **Jai-alai Palace**, located directly across the street from the ferry terminal. This was once an arena *(frontón)* for the lightning-fast Basque ball game of jai-alai, but with the promise of greater income from gambling it was converted.

The grandstand situated on the seaside road, the **Avenida da Amizade** (Friendship Avenue), marks the finishing line for the Macau Grand Prix, the international car-racing event held here every November.

Continuing around the peninsula in a clockwise direction brings you to the **Rua da Praia Grande** (Big Beach Street) – a pleasant promenade with shaded benches under the banyan trees. Along this elegant avenue is **Government House**, a modest pink palace.

Tiles in the Leal Senado building

The central square of the historic city centre is **Largo do Senado** (Senate Square). For an authentic feel of old Portugal, slip into the cool entrance hall of the impressive **Leal Senado** (Loyal Senate) building, a fine example of colonial architecture. On the inside walls are flowered blue tiles *(azulejos)* and coats of arms. The inscription over the archway reads, *'Cidade do nome de Deus, não ha outra mais leal'* ('City of the Name of God, None is More Loyal') – praise for Macau's loyalty during the Spanish occupation of Portugal in the 17th century when the enclave refused to fly the aggressor's flag. Completed in 1876, the building was restored in 1939, with further internal restoration done in the late 20th century. For all its historic grandeur, the Loyal Senate now is the equivalent of a city council, its statesmanship dedicated to water supplies, sewers and the establishment of playgrounds.

➤ Macau's most memorable monument is the Baroque façade of the ruins of **São Paulo** (St Paul's), the only remains of a beautiful 17th-century Jesuit church. On top of a hill in the centre of the city, it's approached by a grand staircase. The rest of the building and an adjoining college were destroyed in a typhoon-fanned fire in 1835. The rich sculptural effects on the façade mix Eastern and Western symbols: familiar saints, Chinese dragons and a Portuguese caravel. Beneath the church, the Museum of Sacred Art houses a collection of sacramental objects.

The ambitious **Museum of Macau** (open Tues–Sun 10am– 6pm; admission fee) opened in 1998 in the lower levels of the **Monte Fortress**. Entrance is by escalator, near St Paul's. The museum gives an overview of Macau's history and its daily life and traditions. A re-created street of colonial

Macau Essentials

Shopping: Like Hong Kong, Macau is a duty-free port. It is famous for its gold jewellery. Market prices per *tael* (34g/1.2oz) of gold are set daily. You should always ask for a certificate of guarantee when you buy gold or jewellery. Look for jewellery shops along Avenida do Infante D Henrique and Avenida de Almeida Ribeiro.

Shops aimed at the tourist market are interspersed with the more workaday ironmongers, herbalists and noodle stalls. Knowledgeable visitors look for antiques – either Chinese heirlooms or remnants from the Portuguese colonial days. However, you are not likely to find bargains, and you should be aware that unless you are an expert, you can end up with a fake. Also worth investigating are contemporary handicrafts, both Portuguese and Chinese, from across the border.

Dining: Macau's own cuisine is a combination of Chinese cooking styles and ingredients infused with flavours imported from Portugal, Brazil and Africa. Whether you choose to dine in one of the Macanese, Chinese, traditional Portuguese, or international-style restaurants, you will be treated to a hearty meal at a good price.

Fresh fish and seafood is particularly good. A delicate, delicious fish is Macau sole *(linguado)*. Imported dried cod *(bacalhao)* is the Portuguese national dish; several varieties are available in local restaurants, usually baked.

Macau has an ample supply of Portuguese wines. Try a *vinho verde*, a mildly sparkling young wine from northern Portugal, or a hearty red Dão or Colares. After dinner, a glass of Madeira or port is recommended to round off the meal.

Cannon at Monte Fortress

Macau is lined with traditional Chinese shops. The fort, built by the Jesuits in the 17th century as a defence against the Dutch, was largely destroyed by the same fire that burned St Paul's.

Luís Vaz de Camões (1524–80), the Portuguese national poet whose work immortalised that country's golden age of discoveries, may have stayed in Macau. Local legend claims that he wrote part of his great saga, *Os Lusíadas*, in what is now called the **Camões Grotto**, situated in the spacious tropical Camões Garden.

Next to the museum, behind a gate (opened to anyone who knocks), is the **Old Protestant Cemetery**. Those whose fate was to die on some far foreign field could not have wanted a more peaceful, lovely graveyard. The small, whitewashed chapel was the first Protestant church built in China.

For a different vision of Old China, visit the classic **Lou Lim Ieoc Garden**. Here, arched bridges, pagodas, fish ponds and stands of bamboo create the mood of a timeless Chinese painting. Nearby is the **Memorial House of Dr Sun Yat-sen**, founder of the Chinese Republic. Photos and documents tell the life story of the physician-statesman, who lived for a time in Macau, but never in this building.

Kun Iam Tong, off Avenida do Coronel Mesquita (open daily 8am–6pm), is a 17th-century Buddhist temple of considerable splendour and charm. Surrounded by statues, carvings and incense burners, here the faithful make their devotions and check their fortunes, and traditional funerary displays give a cheerful send-off to the recently departed.

An unexpected piece of historical memorabilia turns up in the monastery garden, where guides point out a small stone table used for a treaty-signing ceremony in 1844. The signatories, who were the Chinese viceroy from Canton and the minister plenipotentiary of the United States of America, put their names to a historic document – the first-ever treaty between the two countries.

On the swathe of reclaimed land southwest of the jetfoil terminal is the **Macau Cultural Centre**, with two auditoria, galleries, conference hall and dance and music studios. The adjacent **Museum of Art** (open Tues–Sun 10am–7pm; small admission), houses a collection of over 3,000 works. Nearby, dominating the skyline on a small man-made causeway stands the 20-m (66-ft) bronze **statue of Kun Iam**, sculpted by Portuguese artist Christina Reira. Underneath, in the dome-shaped lotus, there's a small meditation centre and library.

The 17th-century Buddhist temple of Kun Iam Tong

Perched on a rather bleak point at the seaside edge of the Nam Van Lakes is the **Macau Tower**, stretching 338m (1,109ft) above the city and opened in 2001. You can take a lift to the observation tower (HK$70 adult) for panoramic views, and if you are brave you can walk over glass floor panels which give vertiginous views of the ground 223m (732ft) straight down. There's a revolving restaurant on top of the tower, and in the adjoining convention centre you'll find a shopping plaza, more restaurants and a cinema.

Macau's oldest museum, the **Maritime Museum** (open Wed–Mon 10am–5.30pm; admission fee) traces the history of Macau's connection to the sea. Exhibits cover fishing, seaborne trade, sea transport, and there is an aquarium. The museum also offers boat tours aboard a fishing junk.

The museum is almost on the spot where the Portuguese first landed. When they came ashore they found the **A-Ma Temple** (properly called Ma Kok Temple; open daily dawn to dusk), dedicated to the favourite goddess of fishermen, who is also known as Tin Hau. The area was called A-Ma Gau ('Bay of A-Ma'), and in this way, Macau got its name. The ornate, picturesque temple dates from the Ming Dynasty (1368–1644) and is the oldest building in Macau.

The remains of the 17th-century **Barra Fortress**, which once defended the southern tip of the peninsula, contains the chapel of **Santiago** (St James). The saint is much revered in the area. Among other legends surrounding the statue is a very modern one: during the Cultural Revolution, when Red Guards were running rampant on nearby Wanchai island, the image of St James is said to have stepped down from the altar and halted an invasion. Part of the fortress is now used as a hotel. The northernmost point in Macau is the frontier between two contrasting worlds. The Barrier Gate *(Portas do Cerco)*, which was built more than a century ago, marks the boundary between the enclave of Macau and the People's Republic of China.

Trying Your Luck

Macau's casinos are a source of non-stop excitement. There are 12 of them; you can't miss the eye-popping **Lisboa**, which has several floors of gambling, but there's also the **Hyatt Regency** and the **Mandarin Oriental**. The fancifully decorated **Macau Palace**, a floating casino moored on the western waterfront, is fitted out with gambling tables, slot machines (known locally as 'hungry tigers') and a restaurant. Gambling is wildly popular with the Chinese of Hong Kong, and they make up nearly 80 percent of all visitors to the casinos.

There are the familiar international games – baccarat, blackjack, boule, craps, roulette – along with more exotic Chinese pastimes. Watch the *fantan* dealer for a few minutes and you'll almost be an expert: it's simply a matter of how many odd buttons are left after he has divided a pile of them into groups of four.

Doorman at the Lisboa

Dai-Siu (Big and Small) is a dice game in which the croupier throws three dice inside a glass container. Players bet on the numbers that will come up and on whether the result will be 'big' or 'small'. *Keno* is like bingo: the player chooses numbers before the draw is made.

The casinos have no admission charge and formal dress is optional, though long trousers for men are required. They keep busy 24 hours a day, but if you want a change of scene there are always more gambling opportunities available. You can try your luck at betting on *jai-alai* at the Jai-alai Palace, greyhound-racing at the Canidrome (one of the largest in the world) and harness-racing on Taipa.

Taipa and Coloane

Bridges link Macau with its two islands. Since the construction of the new Macau-Taipa Bridge has allowed easy access to the airport, the population has grown to more than 30,000, with industrial development, new apartment blocks and luxury resort hotels.

The quaint **Taipa Village**, with its narrow lanes and colonial buildings painted yellow, blue and green, has almost been completely swallowed up by the development of nearby housing estates. The island is also the designated home of the

The Macau–Taipa Bridge

University of East Asia. Pay a visit to the **Casa Museu da Taipa** (open Tues–Sun 10am–6pm; admission fee) and you'll be able to get a glimpse of how Macanese families lived in former days. A grand colonial house, fully restored and fitted out with period furnishings, provides the centrepiece for this expanding 'cultural village'.

Further away is **Coloane**, connected to Taipa by a causeway and a large land reclamation project. Not as developed as Taipa, it offers the joys of sand and sea and is known for its beaches. **Cheoc Van Beach** and **Hac Sa Beach** ('Black Sands') are both popular resort areas, with lifeguards on duty in summer and windsurfing boards for hire. There are restaurants, swimming pools and changing facilities.

The village of Coloane is very picturesque, with a central square lined with charming cafés. The waterfront drive runs parallel to the shore of a Chinese island, and boats going to China usually pass through the narrow waterway. The small but interesting **Chapel of St Francis Xavier** is dedicated to the 16th-century patron saint of missionaries.

Seac Pai Van Park, on the west coast of the island, is an interesting natural preserve with a natural history museum.

EXCURSION TO GUANGZHOU (CANTON)

Guangzhou, previously known to Westerners as Canton, was China's major seaport for 2,000 years and the centre for European traders in the 19th century. The city still maintains its important gateway role. Ever since 1957 the Canton Trade Fair (Chinese Export Commodities Fair) has attracted throngs of international business people every spring and autumn.

Guangzhou, with a population of more than 5 million, straddles the Zhu Jiang, or Pearl River – China's fifth longest – which skirts the city on its western and southern sides and links it to the South China Sea. This waterway accounts for much of the local charm and excitement, as the daily drama of the ferry-boats, junks, sampans, freighters – and even small tankers and big gunboats – unfolds right in the centre of town. The river also irrigates the carefully tended surrounding farmlands, creating a lush, subtropical scene. Guangdong Province has some of China's most fertile land, and grows two crops of rice a year, along with vegetables of all kinds.

Guangzhou is one of China's most prosperous cities, determinedly on the move into the modern world. Thanks to rapid urbanisation, the picturesque older sections with their old houses, narrow streets and winding alleyways may not be around for much longer.

Arriving in Guangzhou

There are many package tours to Guangzhou from Hong Kong *(see page 112)*, and this may be the easiest way to visit the city. However, it's also easy to get to Guangzhou by train or ferry. Seven express trains leave daily from the Kowloon-Canton Railway (KCR) Station in Hung Hom, Kowloon, making the trip in less than two hours. Turbojet craft leave the China Hong Kong City (CHKC) terminal twice a day; the journey takes two hours. The China Travel Service operates a bus route to Guangzhou from just outside the Hung Hom train station, you can buy tickets from any CTS office. There's a bus every hour on average and the journey time is around 3 hours.

You will need a visa to enter China *(see page 108)*. Hong Kong currency is widely accepted in Guangzhou, or you can change your currency into RMB *(yuan)* at any bank or hotel *(see page 117)*. Guangzhou, like Hong Kong, is primarily Cantonese-speaking, but many people also speak Mandarin. English is spoken in hotels and tourist destinations.

If you travel by train, you will arrive at Guangzhou East Station, a large modern complex, which connects with the underground, buses, hotel transfer services and taxis. The station is in the newer business district; nearby is Asia's third-tallest building, Citic Plaza, 391m (1,283ft).

Sights in Guangzhou

Yuexiu Park, Guangzhou

Yuexiu Park, situated near the Trade Fair in the northern part of the city, is Guangzhou's largest; it covers a hilly 100 hectares (250 acres). The park is landscaped with lakes and gardens. On a hilltop in the park is the 1380 **Zhenhailou** (Tower Overlooking the Sea), one of the city's oldest buildings. This five-storey pavilion was built as a memorial to the seven great sea journeys undertaken by the eunuch Zheng He – to East Africa, the Persian Gulf and Java – between 1405 and 1433. Today it contains a fine collection of historical exhibits.

The **Five Rams Statue** stands in the middle of the park. It celebrates the founding of Guangzhou, when five spirits rode their goats down from the celestial realm to present the inhabitants of the city with their very first grains of rice.

Dr Sun Yat-sen's Memorial Hall honours the founder of the Chinese Revolution, flanked by his heroic statue in copper. Dr Sun Yat-sen (1866–1925) began his political career in Canton. This enormous, modern version of a traditional Chinese building, with sweeping blue tile roofs, contains an auditorium big enough to seat 4,700 people. It was built in 1931 with contributions from overseas Chinese.

Guangzhou's most important Buddhist monument is the 1,400-year-old **Liurong Si** (Temple of the Six Banyan Trees) (open daily 8am–5pm). Although the banyan trees that once flourished here are now no more, the often-restored complex

Sun Yat-sen's Memorial Hall

has remained a focus of local Buddhist activities. Golden Buddha statues in several of Buddha's aspects adorn the temples and overlooking them is the 17-storey **Hua Ta**, or Flower Pagoda, a slender relic of the Song dynasty (AD960–1279).

In the early Middle Ages, Canton had a significant Muslim population as a result of its trade with the Middle East. This explains the presence of the Huaisheng Si, or **Huaisheng Mosque** in Guangzhou, reputed to be China's oldest and traditionally dated AD627. Rebuilt in modern times, the mosque serves the small local community of devout Muslims. The modern minaret is known as the **Guang Ta** (Naked Pagoda), in contrast to the Flower Pagoda of the Buddhist Temple of the Six Banyan Trees.

Chen Jia Ci, the Chen Family Temple (open daily 8.30am–5pm), was built in the late 19th century to promote arts and crafts. An architectural wonder, it is itself a beautiful piece of craftsmanship with its sculpture and carved stone balustrades. Porcelain friezes adorn the rooftops and ridgepoles, telling the story of the *Romance of the Three Kingdoms*. Inside is a collection of ceramics, carvings and furniture. There is also a market and a porcelain shop.

Further north off Jiefang Bei Lu is the **Nanyue Wangmu** (Museum of the Western Han; open daily 9am–5.30pm;

admission fee), which recreates the tomb of a Han dynasty emperor dating back more than 2,000 years. The tomb was discovered in 1983, when construction workers were clearing the site to build the China Hotel. Exhibits include skeletons of the emperor and his servants and funeral objects such as jade armour and ornaments.

The atmosphere of 19th-century Canton is best evoked on **Shamian Island**, a haunting, nostalgic place on the Pearl River. This small formerly residential island, beautifully shaded by banyan trees, was the home of the closed community of the foreign colony in the era of 'concessions'. The bridges were barred by night with iron gates to keep the Chinese out. Its stately European-style buildings have since been restored, largely for use as government offices and foreign legations.

A popular optional excursion is an hour's detour to **Guangzhou Zoo** (open daily 8am–5pm; admission fee), founded in 1958. It houses more than 400 animal species, most famous of which is the giant panda, and has an imaginative monkey-shaped mountain behind a moat.

Not to be missed is a visit to Guangzhou's famous open-air market, **Qing Ping**. The Cantonese have the reputation of eating almost anything that lives and breathes, and the market bears this out: along with the usual ducks and chickens, you will see for sale snakes, dogs, bats and sometimes monkeys – all are highly prized as delicacies. More pleasantly, you can browse among lanes of antiques, flowers, herbs, fruit, goldfish, songbirds and other exotica.

Elegant Shamian

Side Trip to Foshan

A very popular day-trip from Guangzhou goes to **Foshan**, a city of nearly 300,000 people, renowned for its handicrafts for more than 1,000 years. The individual artisans' shops are no longer here, but you can visit a silk-weaving factory, a ceramics plant and the **Foshan Folk Art Studio**, where you can observe workers making Chinese lanterns, carving sculptures, painting scrolls and cutting intricate designs in paper. The Foshan Art Porcelain Factory has traditional designs, but also some attractive modern pieces.

Foshan's most outstanding artistic monument is **Zu Miao**, the Taoist Ancestral Temple, a Sung dynasty establishment rebuilt in the 14th century and well worth visiting. Constructed in wood, brick, stone, ceramic and bronze, this is a work of extravagant beauty, uniting many ancient art forms. The complex contains the oldest wooden stage in China, used by the Wan Fu Tai Chinese opera.

EXCURSION TO SHENZHEN

Shenzhen was China's first Special Economic Zone. Literally created out of rural farmland, it was set up in the 1970s as the answer to Hong Kong. From a population of 20,000 it has grown into a metropolis of 2.5 million, with tightly clustered skyscrapers and some of China's highest grossing industries.

Because Shenzhen is much cheaper than Hong Kong, it is a popular weekend destination for Hong Kong's Chinese, who come to relax, dine in its resorts and play golf – Shenzhen hosted the World Cup of Golf in 1995. It is even becoming something of a commuter town – owning or renting an apartment here costs a fraction of what it would in Hong Kong.

Shenzhen is very easy to reach – the KCR commuter train runs throughout the day, the trip taking about 40 minutes. Visitors need a visa to enter China and must disembark at the border (now called 'boundary') checkpoint, Lo Wu. Nine turbojets make the one-hour trip (7.30am–6pm) from Hong Kong's Macau Ferry Terminal to Shekou on the Natau Peninsula, which is part of the economic zone.

Shenzhen is a premier shopping centre, and much cheaper than Hong Kong. It is known for its inexpensive (but well-made) knock-off designer goods. You can use your Hong Kong dollars here, so there's no need to change currency. Some places take credit cards, but cash is better for bargaining. Just across the border is the huge **Lo Wu City** shopping mall, which is within walking distance. There are other shopping malls nearby.

Shenzhen's main tourist attractions are its enormous theme parks. One of them – **Splendid China** (daily 9am–8pm) – purports to show 'all of China in one day'. It contains elaborate replicas of China's chief monuments in impressive detail, including a scaled-down version of the Great Wall. The 24 **China Folk Culture Villages** represent China's ethnic variety; they feature craftspeople in traditional costumes along with folksong and dance performances.

After dark, Shenzhen reverberates with its wild, albeit tawdry, nightlife. Pubs, discos, karaoke lounges and girlie bars abound at **Lo Wu**, near the station, and **Shekou**, a satellite town to the west.

Shopping in Lo Wu City

恭
太
蒲奉敬
神恩
歡迎光臨

WHAT TO DO

SHOPPING

While Hong Kong is no longer the bargain shopping destination it once was, there are still some good buys to be had. Since Hong Kong is a duty-free port and charges no sales tax, goods are cheaper here than in their country of manufacture. On photographic equipment, electronic goods and watches, you avoid the luxury tax payable in your home country. Speciality goods and souvenirs, often handmade, come from Hong Kong and elsewhere in China. Custom-made garments by skillful Hong Kong tailors are still much in demand and cost less than elsewhere for comparable garments. Note that alcohol and tobacco are both exceptions to Hong Kong's duty-free regime and are subject to tax.

You'll find that prices are about the same in Hong Kong Central and Kowloon, and somewhat cheaper in Causeway Bay, which caters to local shopping. Large shops on the fashionable thoroughfares tend to be more expensive than smaller 'family' shops tucked away in the side streets.

Stores do not open until 10am or later, but shopping goes on into the evening, up to 10pm or later. Most shops are open seven days a week. Shops in Central are an exception; they generally close at 7pm and are not open on Sunday. The only holiday on which all commerce comes to a halt is the Chinese New Year in January or February.

The large department stores have fixed prices, but elsewhere you should ask whether there is a discount, especially if you buy several items in one shop. Compare prices before you buy any significant item. Always ask to see the manufacturer's guarantee when purchasing watches, cameras and

The Bun Festival procession on Cheung Chau

Looking for a good buy

audio-visual and electronic equipment. Note that when haggling, the merchant assumes you are prepared to pay cash. If, after concluding a deal, you try to pay with a credit card, he may then boost the price.

Shipping. Many stores will pack and ship purchases. Ask if automatic free insurance is provided. If the goods are very valuable or fragile, it is a good idea to buy an all-risk insurance for the shipment.

Where to Buy

Major shopping areas are Tsim Sha Tsui in Kowloon, especially along Nathan Road; Central on Hong Kong Island, particularly for upmarket designer goods; Causeway Bay for slightly better prices; and the Hollywood Road area for antiques.

Department Stores. Look for Lane Crawford Ltd, an upmarket store with branches at Pacific Place, 70 Queen's Road, and Harbour City; Wing On, one of the oldest in Hong Kong; Marks and Spencer; and the Japanese department stores, Mitsukoshi, Sogo and Seibu.

Malls. Hong Kong is full of giant malls. Harbour City, just west of the Star Ferry Terminal in Tsim Sha Tsui, is one of the largest; Pacific Place, 88 Queensway, is Admiralty's biggest mall, with retail outlets and department stores; Times Square is a collection of retail outlets in Causeway Bay. In addition, most of the top hotels have malls full of designer boutiques.

Factory Outlets. These stores sell excess stock or factory overruns. Hong Kong is no longer a factory outlet centre since much of its clothing manufacturing has moved elsewhere. There are factory showrooms in the Pedder Building, 12 Pedder Street, in Central.

Markets. Markets are the places to use your bargaining skills. Hong Kong's most famous and colourful market is the **Temple Street Night Market** near the Jordan MTR stop. Every conceivable kind of goods is sold here: clothing, all sorts of electronics, CDs, souvenirs, crafts and jewellery.

Stanley Market in Stanley is located on Hong Kong's southern coast, and is well-known for all kinds of clothing, including silk and cashmere. Bargain, and carefully examine any merchandise you buy here.

The **Jade Market**, on Kansu Street in Yau Ma Tei, is known for both jade and freshwater pearls. This is not the place to make expensive purchases, but it's great for inexpensive pendants, earrings and gifts.

Shopping Tips

Be aware that name brands, including electronics, are sometimes fakes, glass may be sold as jade, and that antique you bought may have been made last night. Always ask for a receipt that records information about the item, and if you buy an antique, be sure to get a certificate of authentication. Needless to say, avoid peddlers who approach you in the street.

It is advisable to shop at outlets that are members of the Hong Kong Tourism Board's (HKTB) Quality Tourism Services Scheme, identified by a black Chinese character encircled by a golden letter Q with a small red junk in the bottom left corner. Membership imposes an obligation to maintain standards of both quality and service, and provides dissatisfied customers with an officially recognised channel for redressing complaints; tel: 2806 2823. Pick up a copy of HKTB's *A Guide to Quality Merchants* in which all member stores are listed.

In mid-July, Fashion Week brings parades and events to shopping centres around the city.

What to Buy

Antiques. Hollywood Road in the Mid-Levels above Central is the most famous antiques street in Hong Kong. Look for fine Chinese bronzes, embroidery, lacquerware and porcelain, tomb figures and wood carvings, among other possibilities. The experts point out that it is not age alone that determines a Chinese antique's value – the dynasties of the past had their creative ups and downs. For genuine antiques, try Honeychurch Antiques at No. 29 for furniture and silver, Tai Sing Company at 12 Wyndham Street for porcelain and pottery. For fun you can visit the Low Price Shop at No. 47 or the Cat Street crafts stores and flea market.

Brocades and Silks. Fabrics from China are a bargain and well worth taking home. Chinese-product department stores stock silk fabrics, silk scarves, finely embroidered blouses, and traditional padded jackets. Chinese Arts and Crafts is at Pacific Place in Central, and in Star House in Tsim Sha Tsui; CRC Department Store is on Hennessy Road in Causeway Bay. For fabrics, also try Western Market, Morrison Street, in Sheung Wan.

Cameras. Photo buffs know that Hong Kong is the place to buy some of the world's most advanced photographic equipment, and there are some real bargains around. However, be sure you compare prices and models before buying. Two reliable places to start looking in Lan Kwai Fong are Photo Scientific in the Eurasia Building and Hing Lee Camera Company, 25 Lyndhurst Terrace.

Carpets and Rugs. Hong Kong is a mecca for Chinese hand-knotted wool carpets and silk rugs. Hong Kong's stores are usually able to arrange shipment. Caravan at 65 Hollywood Road and the shops in The Silk Road at Ocean Centre in Tsim Sha Tsui are good places to start looking.

China (porcelain). In Hong Kong you can have a plate, or even a whole dinner service, hand-painted to your own design. Factories in Kowloon and the New Territories, producing traditional and modern china, are geared to entertain and instruct visiting tourists; prices are appealing. A good place to go is the Wah Tung China Company in the Grand Marine Industrial Building in Aberdeen. In antiques shops, look for highly valued porcelains from China. Note that because of the duty-free situation, good bargains may be found in European china, including Spode and Wedgwood.

Electronics. The latest gadgets are sometimes available in Hong Kong before anywhere else. Before you begin shopping, pick up HKTB's *Guide to Quality Merchants* and its visitor pack. Prices on electronics have risen in the past two years; check prices at home before you buy here. Nathan Road has many electronics shops. Also check out Star Computer City in the Star House near the Star Ferry terminal.

Furniture. The choice ranges from traditional hand-carved Chinese rosewood furniture to well-made reproductions of modern Western styles. Rattan furniture is highly popular. Hollywood Road has several furniture shops. Queen's Road East in Wan Chai is a furniture manufacturing and retail area.

Jewels in all shapes and sizes

Jade. 'Good for the health' is just one of the many qualities attributed to these beautiful emerald-green or turquoise stones. Real jade is extremely expensive, and you may be offered counterfeit jade, which looks exactly like the genuine article. Some people say you can test the authenticity by touch – real jade feels smooth and cool. Alternatively, you can shine a lamp on the stone – real jade shows no reflected light. Better still, go shopping with an expert. Kowloon's Jade Market is popular but you are unlikely to pick up any valuable heirlooms here.

Jewellery. Thanks to the duty-free situation, prices in Hong Kong are lower than they are in some other places. You can buy gemstones loose or set, or have them made up to your own design. Popular purchases include diamonds and freshwater pearls. If you do plan to buy jewellery, be sure to consult the *Guide to Quality Merchants* published by the Hong Kong Tourism Board (HKTB) to find a reputable dealer.

Kitchen Equipment. Woks and any other gadgets essential for Chinese cookery make good purchases. Department stores sell all sorts of intriguing kitchen equipment.

Leather Goods. Leather is not a great bargain in Hong Kong. Locally made items do not live up to their European models. However, the leather garment industry is growing, and there is a wide range of locally produced leather acces-

Tailoring

Tailor-made clothes are not as popular in Hong Kong as they were in the past, but hundreds of shops still remain. Local tailors are experts when it comes to producing custom-tailored garments for both men and women, and are also adept at copying patterns. The result can be a quality suit at a fair price – but made-to-measure clothing is not cheap. In choosing a tailor, look for HKTB membership. Many tailors have websites or are listed on websites.

Clothing to suit all tastes in the malls of Hong Kong

sories, all at extremely attractive prices. For European imports, you will pay top dollar.

Musical, Audio and Video Equipment. Hong Kong has a vast range of the most high-tech audio-visual, sound, and screen equipment. Before purchasing, visitors should make sure of compatibility with systems in their own countries. Be sure to look around and compare before buying. Whatever you buy, you may be able to gain a discount.

Clothes. Hong Kong's shops carry almost every recognisable European and many American labels, from top-end designers to the moderately priced or trendy. Nathan Road and Granville Road in Tsim Sha Tsui, Central's shopping malls and Causeway Bay are good places to look. There are still many factory outlet stores, particularly in Wan Chai and Causeway Bay, with reasonable prices. Temple Street market, Ladies' market in Mong Kok and the Lanes in Central sell cheap Chinese-style clothes and tourist T-shirts.

Tea. Chinese department stores sell gift tins of exotic blends. If you want to learn something about tea, go to the Moon Garden Tea House at 5 Hoi Ping Road, Causeway Bay. The owners will brew up a pot so you can taste before making a choice.

Watches. The saying 'Time is money' is quite literally true in Hong Kong. An enormous variety of watch makes and models are on sale. Be sure to get the manufacturer's guarantee stamped or signed if you buy a watch. There are plenty of cheap, counterfeit watches for sale in the tourist markets.

ENTERTAINMENT

Hong Kong is a city that never sleeps; plenty of bars and eating places stay open into the early hours. The Hong Kong Tourism Board stocks two free monthly magazines, *Citylife* and *Where*, which give nightlife and restaurant listings as well as a run-down on what's showing at theatres and cinemas. Otherwise you can simply wander through the maze of neon signs and take your pick. For slightly more objective reviews of bars, restaurants and shows study the City Living section of the *South China Morning Post*, the weekly *HK Magazine* or *BC Magazine* which comes out every two weeks. These last two are handed out free in many bars, restaurants and bookshops. Culture buffs are well catered for, and there is always a varied programme of events, ranging from world-class concerts to local amateur dramatic productions.

Musicians in action

A highlight of the arts calendar is the annual **Hong**

Kong Arts Festival, a three-week dose of international culture in February, with concerts, recitals, plays, jazz, Chinese opera, and innovative productions put on by leading talent from both East and West. Tickets for the shows must be reserved well in advance. The one-month **Legends of China Festival** takes place every October-November. Chinese artists from around the world take part in a variety of stage acts, exhibitions and workshops.

A night with the Hong Kong Ballet

There are more than 30 cinemas in Hong Kong, and the latest Western releases are shown in some of the larger ones. English-language films have Chinese subtitles. Films with Mandarin dialogue also have Chinese subtitles, for the benefit of Cantonese speakers, and sometimes subtitles in English.

The **Hong Kong International Film Festival** takes place in March/April. More than 200 films from all over the world are shown at this two-week event.

The Performing Arts

Performance Venues. The theatres in the **Hong Kong Cultural Centre** in Tsim Sha Tsui are the main venues for concerts and opera. Other performing arts centres are the **City Hall** cultural complex, with exhibition halls and theatres that present concerts, plays and films; the **Hong Kong Academy**

for Performing Arts with two major theatres for dance, drama and concert performances; and the **Hong Kong Arts Centre** in Wan Chai, where both local and visiting groups perform. Other centres for concerts, plays and entertainment are Sha Tin Town Hall and Tsuen Wan Town Hall in the New Territories. Larger arenas, including the Queen Elizabeth Stadium, the Hong Kong Coliseum, and the Ko Shan Theatre in Kowloon play host to various concerts, pop concerts, sporting events and variety shows.

Classical Music. The Hong Kong Chinese Orchestra performs new and traditional works; a wide assortment of traditional and Chinese instruments are featured. The Hong Kong Philharmonic Orchestra was founded in 1975. Under its conductor, Choi Ho-Man, it offers Western classical works and new pieces by Chinese composers in its September-to-June season.

Chinese Opera. Cantonese opera is alive and well in Hong Kong, and the two other forms, Beijing and Kunju, are sometimes presented. To most foreigners, this unique art form is likely to be inscrutable at first exposure, but everyone can appreciate the spectacle and the elaborate, glittering costumes. Although the music may seem strange to the unaccustomed ear, it certainly won't send you to sleep with its loud cymbals and drums.

These opera performers have the look of marionettes

Dance. Hong Kong's three professional dance companies – the Hong Kong Ballet Company, the Hong Kong Dance Company and the newer City Contemporary Dance Company – perform regularly, often at the Hong Kong Academy for Performing Arts.

Theatre. The two leading local troupes, the Chung Ying Theatre Company and the Hong Kong Repertory Theatre, perform in Cantonese; there are also English-language performances at the Fringe Club theatres, Lower Albert Road, in Central.

Puppet Shows. The classic Chinese puppet is the shadow puppet, manipulated behind a screen by three rods, but hand puppet and marionette shows are also on offer, often for free at public parks and playgrounds.

Lan Kwai Fong, just below Hollywood Road, by night

Nightlife

Hong Kong by night can suit any taste – riotous, sedate, raw, or cultured. Note that sometimes there is a cover charge of HK$50 to HK$200 at clubs, which may or may not include a couple of drinks.

There are nightclubs in the principal hotels, with bands, dancing and floor shows. Many restaurants and bars have live music. For live jazz and blues try 48th St Chicago Blues at 2A Hart Avenue, Tsim Sha Tsui. The Fringe Club, 21 Lower Albert Road, Central, is Hong Kong's best-known alternative entertainment venue, with jazz, rock and other live music, in addition to a gallery for visual arts and a relaxing rooftop bar.

Bars with views and live music include Sky Lounge in the Sheraton Hotel and Towers, Tsim Sha Tsui, and Cyrano in the Island Shangri-La in Pacific Place. Pubs are numerous. In Tsim Sha Tsui, Ned Kelly's Last Stand on Ashley Road is an Aussie institution; Delaney's, 71–77 Peking Road, is one of Hong Kong's enduring Irish pubs.

The clubs and bars of Wan Chai, long the centre of seedy nightlife, have become almost respectable. Joe Bananas, 23 Luard Road, is a Wan Chai mainstay for all-night partying. Mes Amis at 81–85 Lockhart Road, has a lively dance floor after 11pm at the weekend. A lot of the raunchy action has moved across the harbour to Tsim Sha Tsui East; this is also where you'll find pricey hostess clubs.

Today's trendy spot is Soho (SOuth of HOllywood) around Hollywood Road, Elgin and Stauton streets. Soho, along with the Lan Kwai Fong area, is popular with chuppies (Hong Kong yuppies) and has a lively bar scene. Causeway Bay also has a variety of bars and clubs. TOTT's, in the Excelsior Hotel, is a restaurant with live music and dancing and a harbour view.

SPORTS

Participant Sports

Beaches. In subtropical Hong Kong you can swim from April to early November. There are more than 40 beaches in

Nightlife Tours

Nightlife tours are offered by a number of companies. The most typical of these are harbour cruises, usually including dinner and dancing on board an air-conditioned floating nightclub. There are evening bus tours that include visits to a restaurant and night spots; some tours combine a Chinese banquet with a visit to an open-air market and the panorama from Victoria Peak.

Jogging in the New Territories

Hong Kong that are free to the public. Most have lifeguards on duty from April to October, changing rooms, toilets and snack stands. On Hong Kong Island, Repulse Bay is the most popular; others are Shek O on the east coast and Stanley and Deep Water Bay on the south coast. They are very crowded, especially on summer weekends. On the outlying islands, Cheung Sha is on Lantau, Tung Wan is on Cheung Chau and Hung Shing Ye and Lo So Shing are on Lamma.

Golf. The Hong Kong Golf Club (tel: 2670 1211) welcomes visitors to its three 18-hole courses at Fanling in the New Territories. The Discovery Bay Golf Club on Lantau island (tel: 2987 7273) has an 18-hole Robert Trent Jones Jr. course, open to visitors on Monday, Tuesday and Friday. Many Hong Kong residents and visitors take the express train to Guangzhou to play at the Guangzhou Luhu Golf and Country Club (tel: 2317 1933 in Hong Kong or 020-8350 7777 in the UK). The 72-par course was designed by Dave Thomas.

Hiking. In the New Territories the famous MacLehose Trail stretches 97km (60 miles) from Sai Kung Peninsula to Tuen Mun. The Lantau Trail is a 69-km (43-mile) circular trail on Lantau Island that begins and ends at Silvermine Bay. Both trails are divided into smaller segments of varying difficulty. Maps of hiking trails are available at the Government Publications Centre, Low Block, Government Offices, 66 Queensway in Central. HKTB also has trail maps and sponsors the Guided Nature Walks, led by rangers, that include hikes in all the different regions of Hong Kong.

Taijiquan (Tai Chi). The HKTB offers free lessons in these exercises that improve concentration and balance, starting at 8am outside the Cultural Centre in Tsim Sha Tsui. Contact the HKTB for more information.

Spectator Sports

Horseracing. All levels of society share a feverish interest in the Sport of Kings. The racing schedule is September to June, and Hong Kong maintains two courses – the older Happy Valley course on Hong Kong Island and the Sha Tin track in the New Territories. The HKTB runs a 'Come Horseracing Tour', which includes entry to the Jockey Club visitors' box and members' enclosure, and a buffet-style meal.

Cricket and Rugby. The Hong Kong International Cricket Series, held in late September, brings teams from all over the world. The Rugby Sevens sees teams come together from all over the world for 15 matches in March or early April.

The races at Sha Tin

FOR CHILDREN

Hong Kong has many attractions that appeal to children of all ages. Hong Kong's many beaches are especially fun for children. Children love riding on Hong Kong's antique trams. A ride on the Peak Tram is sure to provide a thrill, and in the Peak Tower they'll enjoy the Peak Explorer ride and Ripley's Believe it or Not! Odditorium *(see page 29)*.

Traditional dance often takes to the streets during festivals

Ocean Park *(see page 37)* is very popular with children of all ages. There's a dinosaur world, thrilling rides including a ferris wheel and fun animal shows.

Hong Kong's state-of-the-art interactive museums will appeal to children. The Science Museum in Tsim Sha Tsui East allows children to get their hands on more than half of its 500 exhibits, while the nearby Space Museum has regular screenings on an enormous Omnimax screen in its Space Theatre, making the night sky come vibrantly alive.

For children who love boats, riding the Star Ferry or ferry trips to outlying islands will be exciting, and the Dolphin Watch trip *(see page 113)* is certain to appeal. If you plan to visit during May, the carnival atmosphere of the Cheung Chau Bun Festival, with its high bamboo-and-paper towers covered in steamed buns, will fascinate youngsters.

Calendar of Festivals

For the most up-to-date information, consult the Hong Kong Tourism Board, or pick up a free copy of the HKTB's *Hong Kong Diary.* Note that precise dates cannot be given as Chinese festivals are fixed according to the lunar calendar.

January/February: *Lunar New Year* (Spring Festival). Everything in Hong Kong, even businesses, shuts down for three days. This is a time when families traditionally get together. In the days leading up to the festival air fares rise to take advantage of families heading off to visit relatives overseas or choosing to go on holiday. Border controls at Lo Wu are literally jam-packed with families laden down with gifts and food, struggling to reach their home towns in Guangdong province. It is not a good time to visit China. For most people it means an opportunity to clear out the old – houses are spring-cleaned, people have their hair cut, buy new clothes and settle their debts. The occasion is marked with packed flower shows – the biggest one is in Victoria Park. People visit temples and hand *outlai see* (lucky money) packets to children and unmarried friends, accompanied by the words *Kung hei fat cho* (May you prosper in the New Year). There is a parade on the waterfront, and an elaborate fireworks display lights up the harbour.

February: *Spring Lantern Festival (Yuen Siu).* The last day of the Chinese New Year celebrations is also known as Chinese Valentine's Day, since it was traditionally the time when unmarried women donned their finest clothes and ventured out with their chaperones to meet some eligible young men.

April: *Ching Ming Festival.* This Confucian festival, timed to the solar calendar, is one of two annual holidays on which to honour the dead. Ancestors' graves are swept and offerings of food, wine or flowers are made, while gold and silver 'money' is burned to give the ancestors enough to spend in the afterworld.

April/May: *Birthday of Tin Hau.* The Taoist Goddess of the Sea is honoured by fishing communities with prayers for safe voyages and good catches. The liveliest celebration is at Joss House Bay, where decorated junks and sampans converge with offerings. Spectators can reach the beach by spe-

cial excursion boats. Smaller-scale celebrations, including lion-dancing, take place at other Tin Hau temples, notably at Aberdeen.
May: *Birthday of the Lord Buddha.* In Buddhist temples throughout the territory, the Buddha's image is bathed in scented water to symbolise the washing away of sins. *Cheung Chau Bun Festival.* This ritual was apparently initiated when human bones were discovered during construction of the Pak Tai Temple. Fearing that the temple would be haunted by the spirits which had been disturbed, the island's inhabitants sought to appease them by putting out offerings of steamed buns. Today, the event is celebrated by the erection of three 16-m (52-ft) bamboo towers, each piled with some 5,000 pink and white lotus-paste buns. The festival lasts for about eight or nine days; processions, lion and dragon dances and traditional rites at the temple give the island a carnival atmosphere.
May/June: *Dragon Boat Festival (Tuen Ng).* Oarsmen in long, thin dragon boats race to the beat of big bass drums and Chinese gongs. Annual International Dragon Boat races are usually held a few days after the festival in June or July.
July: *Birthday of Lu Pan.* The Taoist patron saint of carpenters and builders is honoured with celebratory banquets.
August: *Seven Sisters' (Maidens') Festival.* A festival for lovers, centered on an old legend. Women praying for husbands leave offerings at Lovers' Rock. *Hungry Ghosts Festival (Yue Lan).* Paper offerings are burned and food left out to placate ghosts who have been temporarily released from the underworld.
September: *Mid-Autumn Festival.* Celebrating the year's harvest, this one is a children's favourite. As the full moon rises, tots carrying paper lanterns of traditional or space-age design congregate in open spaces or high places to admire the poetic sight. They eat moon cakes (ground sesame and lotus seeds or dates, perhaps enriched with duck egg) and take full advantage of being allowed to stay up late.
October: *Cheung Yeung Festival.* Nineteen centuries ago, so it is said, a man visited the hills on the advice of a fortune-teller. When he returned he found he was the sole survivor of a calamity. On the ninth day of the ninth moon, people visit the hillside graves of their ancestors and try to reach some high place for luck.

EATING OUT

The Chinese care about food with a passion only the French can rival. For the Chinese, eating is a pleasure imbued with philosophical profundities: even the dead are offered food and wine to make their journey from this life more peaceful.

Chinese restaurants are a place for family and social gatherings. Eating out is one of the main forms of socialising, and the Chinese usually eat in large groups. The food is best enjoyed if there is a variety of dishes. If Chinese hosts invite you to a restaurant, put yourself in their hands; they will try to order according to their impression of your tastes.

A common Cantonese greeting is '*Lay sik jaw fan may ah*?' – ('Have you had your rice yet?')

Chefs have a demanding clientele. Chinese gourmets demand the freshest food from local farms and the sea – they require not only the best flavours but colour, texture and presentation to enhance the pleasure of the food. A proper Chinese meal is orchestrated, and must contain a harmonious progression from sweet to sour, crunchy to tender. A Chinese banquet is a triumph of the well-rounded art of food.

You rarely find a bad Chinese meal here. The big problem is how to choose from among the thousands of restaurants, and then among the hundreds of items on the menu. Let the waiter help you to choose just the right amount of food with the best range of tastes and textures.

In Hong Kong you'll find restaurants offering cuisines from all over Asia, and a wide choice of Western cuisines, especially French but also Italian, Dutch, and Mexican, as well as steak, pizza and kosher food. Vegetarians do not have an easy time in Hong Kong. Most Chinese chefs use chicken or other meat stock routinely in otherwise vegetarian dishes, but there are a handful devoted to a purely vegetarian cuisine.

Meal Times

Most hotels serve a breakfast buffet of Chinese and Western food from about 7 to 10am. At lunchtime business people pack the restaurants from 1 to 2.30pm. Dinner is between 7.30 and 9.30pm, but Chinese restaurants are flexible; many are open from early in the morning until midnight without a break.

A traditional Chinese breakfast consists of *congee*, a rice gruel or porridge to which almost anything may be added. At back-street breakfast stalls you'll also see the early risers digging into noodle soup with chunks of vegetable or pork.

A breakfast chef at the Harbour Plaza Hotel

Regional Cuisines

Chinese food comes in half a dozen principal styles, all very different from one another. In Hong Kong every major school of Chinese cooking is represented; restaurants have inherited recipes and brilliant cooks from all parts of China.

Cantonese

For visitors, this is probably the most familiar Chinese cuisine, as so many Can-

The colour of Cantonese cuisine

tonese emigrated, opened restaurants, and introduced new tastes to diners in the West. Cantonese food is either steamed or stir-fried, cooking methods that capture the natural flavour of the ingredients as well as the colour and vitamins. A vast range of ingredients is used, and the flavours are many and often delicately understated.

Garoupa, a delicious local fish, comes steamed in the company of ginger, spring onions and soy sauce, with a touch of garlic. Prawns come in a sauce of sugar, vinegar, soy and ketchup, coloured with the addition of crisp red and green peppers and pineapple chunks. Lemon chicken consists of fried chunks of tender chicken in a creamy sauce of sugared lemon juice and chicken broth. A hearty soup is crabmeat and corn soup; soup is usually served towards the end of the meal. Steamed white rice is normally served with a Cantonese meal.

Chiu Chow

This regional cuisine from the Swatow region of southeast China excels in novel seasonings and rich sauces. Chefs also pride themselves on their amazing vegetable carvings that are part of every Chiu Chow banquet. Before and after dinner you will be presented with tiny cups of a strong and bitter tea, known as Iron Buddha.

Two very expensive Chiu Chow delicacies are shark's fin and bird's nest. A typical dish is minced pigeon: the pigeon meat is minced and fried with herbs, and eaten wrapped in lettuce leaves. In Chiu Chow restaurants *congee* (rice porridge) is often served instead of rice.

Beijing (Peking)

The Chinese emperors made Beijing the gourmet centre of the country, and Hong Kong's Peking restaurants still present truly imperial banquets (ordered in advance) with everything from nuts to soup, in that order. Northern food tends to be richer than Cantonese food. Don't miss the dramatic smashing of the clay around 'beggar's chicken', or one of the world's most delicious eating experiences, Peking duck. The duck is honey-coated before roasting and is cut at the table. The celebrants put chunks of the crisp skin along with spring onions and a sweet sauce, onto delicate pancakes, which are then rolled up and

Chinese dining offers a wide variety of experiences, from humble street food to gourmet cuisine with a view

Freshly roasted duck at a market stall

devoured. The meat is then taken away to be stir fried with other ingredients and served as a separate dish.

Wheat, not rice, is the staple food in northern China. Peking restaurants serve noodles and various kinds of bread. They also specialise in wonderful dumplings, stuffed with meat or vegetables and prepared by steaming or frying.

Shanghai

Shanghai restaurants also serve a dish known as 'beggar's chicken'. According to legend, the inventor was a tramp who stole a chicken but had no way to cook it. After tossing in some salt and onion, he covered the entire bird in a shell of mud, then roasted it on a fire. When the mud was baked dry and he smashed the coating – the feathers came off with the clay and all the juicy tenderness of the bird remained. The recipe has become more sophisticated as mushrooms, pickled cabbage, shredded pork, bamboo shoots and wine are added to the stuffing.

Shanghai food is an amalgam of a number of Chinese cuisines from surrounding cities. It tends to be more diverse and complicated as well as more thoroughly cooked than, say, Cantonese. Chili peppers, garlic, and ginger are used in moderation. Freshwater hairy crab, imported from Shanghai in autumn, steamed and eaten with the hands, is a popular dish as is *xiao long bao*, a Chinese-style bun filled with a mixture of minced pork, ginger, spring onion and sesame oil. Shanghai diners usually prefer noodles to rice.

Sichuan

This food from southwestern China has become popular in America. It produces such sharp, hot flavours that it first takes your breath away, then awakens your palate. Once the fiery shock of the garlic-enhanced peppers has subsided, you can distinguish the other many elements in unlikely coexistence – bitter, sweet, fruity, tart and sour.

Smoked duck, Sichuan style, is marinated in rice wine, with ginger and an array of spices, then steamed before being smoked over a specially composed wood fire. Equally delicious is deep-fried beef with vegetables, a dish in which the meat and most of the other ingredients – carrots, celery, peppers, garlic – are shredded and slowly fried over a low flame.

All Chinese foods are pleasing to the eye, but there are some Sichuan foods that appeal to the ear. 'Thunder' dishes are topped with crisp rice, which sizzles and pops on contact with the other ingredients.

Try Chopsticks

You'll lose face – and fun – if you don't learn to use chopsticks to eat your food in Hong Kong. There's no reason to feel self-conscious – the Chinese are tolerant when it comes to table manners.

Begin by settling the bottom stick firmly at the conjunction of the thumb and forefinger, balancing it against the first joint of the ring finger. The second stick pivots around the fulcrum made by the tip of the thumb and the inside of the forefinger.

Remember not to lay your chopsticks across each other, and never place them across the rice bowl, but rest them on the holder provided or against a plate.

Forks and knives are supplied in most restaurants. If it's any consolation, many Chinese don't feel quite at home with them either.

Hakka

The name Hakka means 'guest people', referring to their migration to this region from northern China many centuries ago. Hakka cuisine involves the use of simple ingredients, especially versatile bean curd. Look for an ingenious dish called salted chicken; a coating of salt contains and increases the flavours while the bird is being baked.

Dim Sum

Late breakfast or lunch can consist of tea and *dim sum*, the small snacks which add up to a delicious, filling meal. Servers wander from table to table chanting the Cantonese names of the foods contained in bamboo steamers on their trays or carts. Choose whatever looks interesting – from spring rolls to spare ribs and dozens of different dumpling varieties, including: *siu mai* (pork and shrimp dumplings), *har gau* (delicate steamed

Dim Sum includes dozens of different dumpling varieties

shrimp dumplings), and *cha siu bau* (barbecued pork buns). When you ask for the bill, the waiter will count the number of empty dishes on the table and tot up the bill.

The famous 'thousand-year eggs' are duck eggs buried in lime for 60 days, with a resulting cheese-like taste.

Drinks

The Chinese having a dinner party at the table next to you are probably drinking Cognac with their meal. Hong Kong claims the world's highest per capita consumption of brandy, possibly because of a vague belief that it has aphrodisiac qualities. European and Australian table wines are also available, and they are now relatively inexpensive.

Few visitors develop a taste for Chinese wines, despite their 4,000-year history. Some are too sweet, others too strong. Unlike the Chinese grape and rice wines, the wheat-based wines are notorious for their alcoholic power. Mao Tai is a breathtaking case in point.

The best choice for the visitor is beer. The locally brewed San Miguel is cheap and refreshing. Tsingtao beer from China has a hearty European taste. You'll also find a large selection of European brands, some of them brewed locally under licence.

The Chinese have been drinking tea for many centuries as a thirst-quencher, general reviver, and ceremonial beverage. Tea in China is drunk without sugar or milk, although English-style tea is available in hotels. It's worth making the effort to learn to appreciate the many varieties of tea and their histories. For a caffeine-free alternative, ask for hot chrysanthemum tea, brewed from the dried petals of the flower.

Rounding off the beverage list are familiar soft drinks and tasty tropical fruit juices. Most hotels serve excellent coffee at breakfast, and it is also available in snack bars.

To Help You Order...

Waiter!/Waitress!	**Mgoi!**
Have you a table?	**Yau mo toi ah?**
Do you have a set menu?	**Yau mo to chaan a?**
I'd like a/an/some...	**Ngor seung yiu...**
The bill, please.	**Mai dan, m goi.**

beer	**bei jau**	ice	**bing**
beef	**ngau yuk**	lamb	**yurng yuk**
cake	**daan go**	menu	**chan pye**
chicken	**gai**	pork	**ju-ee yuk**
chopsticks	**fai ji**	rice	**faan**
cup	**bui**	steak	**ngau pa**
dessert	**tim bun**	soup	**tong**
fish	**yue**	tea	**cha**
fruit	**sang gwo**	water	**sui**
glass	**bor lay bui**	wine	**jau**

...and Read the Menu

bean curd and crabmeat soup	蟹肉荳腐羹
bean curd with pork in pepper sauce	麻婆荳腐
diced chicken with walnuts	合桃鷄丁
diced pork with cashew nuts	腰果肉丁
fried bamboo shoots and cabbage	干燒冬筍
fried eel with soya sauce	炒鱔糊
fried shrimps	淸炒蝦仁
fried sliced pork with green pepper	青椒肉絲
mushrooms with vegetables	菜扒鮮菇
shredded chicken with green pepper	辣子鷄丁
sliced beef with green pepper and bean sauce	豉椒牛肉
sliced chicken, abalone and prawn soup	三絲湯
sliced fish with brown sauce	紅燒魚片
stewed yellow fish	糟溜黃魚
sweet and sour pork	咕嚕肉
Tientsin cabbage and asparagus	鷄油津白

HANDY TRAVEL TIPS

An A–Z Summary of Practical Information

A

ACCOMMODATION (see also RECOMMENDED HOTELS, page 128)

Most of Hong Kong's more than 35,000 hotel rooms are in luxury or first-class hotels, so finding moderately-priced or budget accommodation is not always easy. Hong Kong's high seasons are October to early December, and March and April. In other months, particularly in summer, prices may drop, and bonuses such as upgrades, free airport transport and discounts may be offered.

The price of a room in Hong Kong often depends upon its view. For the best rates, check with a travel agent or look for a package that offers hotel and airfare. Rooms tend to be small except in the most expensive places. High- and mid-range hotels are all members of the Hong Kong Tourism Board (HKTB); check for membership in this organisation when booking an inexpensive accommodation.

Advance reservations are essential for moderately-priced hotels, and advisable for all others. For visitors arriving without reservations, the Hotel Reservation Centre at the airport can arrange a room at any of the hotels affiliated with the Hong Kong Hotels Association; the service is provided free of charge and the desk is open from 8am–midnight.

Hong Kong hotels include all the major international chains. Many of the more modest establishments offer services comparable to first-class hotels. Posted rates cover the room price only; a 10 percent service charge and a 3 percent government tax are added to the bill at check-out time.

AIRPORT

Arriving. International flights land at the Chek Lap Kok Airport, just off Lantau Island, <www.hkairport.com>. Immigration and customs checks are efficient in this modern airport. Beyond the baggage inspection area you will find a bank, money changers, the Hotel Reservation Centre desk and the information counter of the

Hong Kong Tourism Board. The Ground Transportation Centre is the place to go for information about transportation into the city, or for taxis and limousine service.

Airport Express (AEL). (tel: 2881 8888) This rail link is the quickest and most efficient way to get into the city. Trains run every 10 minutes from 5.50am–1.15am daily to Kowloon (20 minutes travel time) and Hong Kong Central (23 minutes) stations where there is free shuttle bus service to many hotels. Buy tickets from the automatic machines.

Airport Shuttle Service. (tel: 2377 0733) The deluxe bus runs every 30 minutes from 6.15am–12.15am, door-to-door to most hotels; book at counters A16 or B16 in the arrival hall.

Airbuses. (tel: 2873 0818) The buses serve all major hotels. Take A21 to Kowloon, All and A12 to Hong Kong Island. Travel time is about an hour. Buy tickets at the Commercial Service Counter or have exact fare ready.

Limousines and Taxis. Major hotels operate their own limousine services; go to the Hotel Reservation Centre if you have a reservation, or look for the hotel pick-up counters. If you take a taxi, you should be charged only what the meter reads, plus tolls and a charge for each piece of luggage placed in the boot.

Departure. Most major airlines, including Cathay Pacific, United and Singapore Airlines, allow you to check in for your return flight at either Hong Kong Central Station or Kowloon Station up to 24 hours before your departure. Boarding passes will be issued, and luggage transferred to the airport.

B

BUDGETING FOR YOUR TRIP

To give you an idea of what to expect in terms of cost, here are some average prices in Hong Kong dollars. However, remember that prices change, so they should be regarded as approximate.

Airport Transfer. Limousine from the airport to your hotel, about HK$500; taxis HK$250–$400, plus tolls and luggage; Airport Express HK$90–$100; Airport Shuttle HK$120; Airbus HK$35–$45.

Buses and trams. Buses HK$1.20–$45, trams HK$2 for adults, HK$1 for children, minibuses and maxicabs HK$2–$22.50, Peak Tram HK$20 (one way), HK$30 (return) for adults, HK$6 (one way), HK$9 (return) for children.

Car rental. A compact car costs around HK$750 a day. A car or limo with a driver costs around HK$160 an hour.

Ferries. Star Ferry HK$1.70–$2.20; island ferries HK$14–$27; Macau ferry HK$130–$247.

Hotels. Luxury hotels range upwards from HK$2,500, top hotels from HK$1,800; medium range hotels begin at around HK$950, and inexpensive hotels less than HK$950. All add 10 percent service charge and 3 percent government tax to the bill.

MTR. Mass Transit Railway fares are HK$4–$26, depending on distance.

Meals and drinks. In a moderately-priced restaurant: set lunch HK$80–$150, dinner HK$150–$350; buffets are generally good value for money.

Taxis. HK$15 for the first 2km (1.2 miles), HK$1.40 for each succeeding 200m, HK$20 for journeys via Cross Harbour Tunnel or HK$30 via the Eastern Harbour Crossing (to cover driver's return toll), and HK$5 for each piece of baggage.

Trains. KCR from Kowloon to the boundary with China, first class HK$66, standard class HK$33.

C

CAR HIRE (See also DRIVING)

Driving in Hong Kong is not recommended. Traffic can be a nightmare, streets are narrow and crowded, and parking often nearly impossible. Hong Kong's public transport system is so good that driving is never as convenient as the MTR or a bus. Moreover, distances are short, and walking is often an easy option.

All international and many local car hire firms operate in Hong Kong offering both self-drive and chauffeur-driven cars. Japanese, European and American models are available.

Major credit cards are accepted. To hire a car, drivers must be over 25 years old and have held a valid licence from their home country or an international licence for two years.

CLIMATE

The best time to visit Hong Kong is in October or November, when the temperature and humidity drop and days are clear and sunny. From December until late February you'll find the air moderately cool with the humidity still low (around 73 percent). In spring the humidity and temperature start rising. March and April can be very pleasant, but from May to mid-September it's extremely hot and often wet, with most of the annual rainfall recorded during these months.

The following chart gives an idea of the average monthly temperatures in Hong Kong, and the number of rainy days per month.

	J	F	M	A	M	J	J	A	S	O	N	D
°C	15	15	18	22	25	28	28	28	27	25	21	17
°F	59	59	64	72	77	82	82	82	81	77	70	63
Days of Rain	6	8	11	12	16	21	19	17	14	8	6	5

CLOTHING

From May to September lightweight summer clothing is called for, and a raincoat and umbrella might come in handy. In restaurants and hotels, beware of the air-conditioning, which can reduce the temperature substantially. From late September to early December shirt-sleeves and sweaters are appropriate, while in winter – late December to February – a wool suit and a warm jacket or light coat are advisable.

Informality is generally the rule in dress. For sightseeing and shopping, virtually any fashion is appropriate. Shorts and T-shirts are perfectly acceptable, but shorts and halter tops are out of place at the more upmarket restaurants and in Chinese temples. You'll see people in formal business attire in Hong Kong's Central business district. Bring along comfortable shoes for the steep slopes of Hong Kong.

CRIME AND SAFETY (See also EMERGENCIES and POLICE)

Hong Kong is a safe city, night and day. The streets are usually full of people until late at night. Signs everywhere warn you to 'beware of pickpockets'. This particularly applies to crowded areas, and Hong Kong has some of the most crowded places you've ever seen. Be especially careful in crowded markets such as the Temple Street Night Market, and on rush-hour buses and MTR trains. It is best to leave your valuables in a hotel safe.

However, you should be aware that there are some safety concerns in Macau. Although these are not likely to affect tourists, Macau has had a recent history of gang warfare.

CUSTOMS AND ENTRY REQUIREMENTS

For most nationalities, only a passport is required for entry into Hong Kong. Subjects of the UK can stay up to six months without a visa; Canadians, Australians and New Zealanders and US citizens can stay for three months. To enter Macau, only a passport is needed, and most visitors can stay up to 20 days without a visa.

Visas are required for entry into the People's Republic of China, so if you are visiting Guangzhou, Shenzhen, or taking any other excursion over the border, you will need a visa. Short-term tours to China include visas; otherwise visas can be arranged at the office of China Travel Service (CITS), 27-33 Nathan Road, Tsim Sha Tsui.

You can bring into Hong Kong duty-free: 200 cigarettes or 50 cigars or 250 grams tobacco, and 1 litre spirits or 1 litre wine.

Firearms are strictly controlled, and can only be brought in by special permit. There are no currency restrictions.

When returning home, duty-free quotas are as follows. Australia: A$400 worth of merchandise, 250 cigarettes or 250 grams tobacco and 1 litre spirits or 1 litre wine. Canada: Can$500 worth of merchandise, 200 cigarettes, 400 grams tobacco, 50 cigars, 1.4 litres spirits and 1.4 litre wine. New Zealand: NZ$700 worth of merchandise, 200 cigarettes or 50 cigars or 250 grams tobacco and 1.1 litres spirits and 4.5 litres wine. UK: £145 worth of merchandise, 200 cigarettes or 50 cigars or 250 grams tobacco and 1 litre spirits and 2 litres wine. US: US$400 worth of merchandise, 200 cigarettes and 100 cigars, 1 litre wine or spirits; Cuban cigars, plants or fresh foodstuffs are prohibited; antiques over 100 years old are duty-free.

D

DRIVING (see also CAR RENTAL)

Anyone over 18 with a valid licence and third-party insurance can drive in Hong Kong for 12 months without having to pay for a local licence. Drivers must carry a valid driver's licence and photo identification at all times.

Road Conditions. Congestion is a serious problem in the city, sometimes leading to impatient driving. Beware of inattentive pedestrians. Good highways connect to the New Territories and the airport.

Rules and Regulations. As in Britain and Australia, Hong Kong traffic keeps to the left. All passengers in private cars, front and back, are required to wear seatbelts. Drivers may not use hand-held mobile phones while driving. Note that across the border in China, as in Europe and the US, cars keep to the right. The speed limit is 30mph (50km/h) in towns, elsewhere as marked.

Parking. This can be a headache, especially in central areas, despite the multi-storey car parks. In busy streets, meters operate from 8am to midnight Monday–Saturday, and wardens are ever alert.

Breakdowns. Telephone the agency from which you hired the car. In an emergency, dial 999 for the police. The Automobile Association is at 391 Nathan Road, Yau Ma Tei, tel: 2739 5273.

Road Signs. Most road signs in Hong Kong are the standard international pictographs.

The following words may help you in explaining your problems to non-English-speaking Chinese:

E

ELECTRICITY

Standard voltage in Hong Kong is 220-volt, 50-cycle AC. Many hotels have razor fittings for all standard plugs and voltages. For other units, transformers and plug adapters will be needed; you may need a plug for your laptop even if it is equipped to deal with both 220 and 110 volts. Most hotels supply hairdryers.

EMBASSIES AND CONSULATES

Consulates are generally open Monday–Friday, 9am–noon and 2–4 or 5pm. Various sections may be open at different hours; to make sure, telephone first.

Australia: 23rd–24th floors, Harbour Centre, 25 Harbour Road, Wan Chai, tel: 2827 8881.

Canada: 12th–14th floors, Tower 1, Exchange Square, 8 Connaught Place, Central, tel: 2810 4321.

New Zealand: 65th floor, Central Plaza, 18 Harbour Road, Wan Chai, tel: 2525 5044.

UK:1 Supreme Court Road, Central, tel: 2901 3000.

US: 26 Garden Road, Central, tel: 2523 9011.

EMERGENCIES

Dial 999 for Police, Fire, or Ambulance departments. St John's Ambulance Brigade is a free service, tel: 2576 6555 on Hong Kong island, 2713 5555 in Kowloon, or 2639 2555 in the New Territories. Hospitals with 24-hour emergency services are: Queen Mary Hospital, 102 Pokfulam Road, Hong Kong Island, tel: 2855 3838; Queen Elizabeth Hospital, 30 Gascoigne Road, Kowloon, tel: 2958 8888; and Hong Kong Adventist Hospital, 40 Stubbs Road, Hong Kong Island, tel: 2574 6211. Many hotels have doctors on call.

In Macau, tel: 573333 for the police and tel: 572222 for fire.

There's been an accident	**Yow yee oy**
collision	**Jong che**
flat tire	**Bow tai**
Help!	**Gau meng ah!**
Police!	**Geng tsa!**

G

GAY AND LESBIAN TRAVELLERS

Hong Kong is still fairly conservative, despite a softening of anti-gay attitudes since the 1991 Crimes Ordinance that de-criminalised homosexual acts. There's a gay scene around Glenealy and Wyndham streets in Central and along Jaffe Road in Wan Chai. The web site for gay nightlife information is <www.gaystation.com.hk>.

GETTING THERE

From North America. Several airlines offer direct flights between North American cities and Hong Kong. Hong Kong's Cathay Pacific Airways (tel: 800/233-2742 <www.cathaypacific.com> has a daily nonstop service from Los Angeles, Vancouver, and Toronto, and direct service, with a stop in Vancouver, from New York. Nonstop flights are also offered by Continental Airlines (tel: 800/525-0280 <www.continental.com>) with daily flights from Newark, NJ; Canadian Airlines International (tel:800/426-7000 <www.cdnair.ca>), with daily flights from Vancouver; Singapore Airlines (tel: 800/742-3333 <www.singaporeair.com>) with daily service from San Francisco; and United Airlines (tel: 800/241-6522; <www.united.com>), with daily nonstop service from JFK New York, Chicago, San Francisco and Los Angeles.

Airlines with direct flights from North America include Northwest Airlines (tel: 800/225-2525; <www.nwa.com>), which also flies to Macau; Japan Airlines (tel: 800/525-3663 japanair.com); Korean Air (tel: 800/438-5000; <www.koreanair.com>). China Airlines (tel: 800/227-5118; <www.china-airlines.com>) flies daily from New York with a change in Taipei.

From the UK. CathayPacific (tel: 020/7747 8888), British Airways (tel: 0845/773 3377; <www.britishairways.com>), and Virgin Atlantic Airways (tel: 01293/747747; <www.virgin.com>) offer daily nonstop services from London to Hong Kong.

From Australia and New Zealand. Both Qantas (tel 131313 <www.qantas.com.au>) and Cathay Pacific (tel: 131747) offer daily nonstop services from Sydney and Melbourne. From New Zealand, Cathay Pacific (tel: 0508/800454) flies daily from Auckland.

GUIDES AND TOURS

There are all kinds of organised tours in Hong Kong, from orientation tours of the city, night cruises of the harbour, and tours of the islands to trips farther afield to Macau, Shenzhen, and Guangzhou.

The Hong Kong Tourism Board (HKTB) organises a large assortment of tours. Tour operators include Gray Line Tours of Hong Kong Ltd., 5/F 72 Nathan Road, Tsim Sha Tsui (tel: 2368 7111); Watertours, at Shop 5C, Ground Floor, Star House, Tsim Sha Tsui (tel: 2926 3868), is the largest operator of boat and junk cruises; Splendid Tours and Travel Ltd (tel: 2316 2151) has night cruises among its offerings; and China Travel Service of Hong Kong Ltd (CITS) runs 1–3-day tours of Guangzhou and other South China destinations.

Most interesting for the visitor who has a few days in Hong Kong are the theme tours sponsored by HKTB. Outstanding is the 'Heritage Tour', which takes you to historic sites in the New Territories. 'The Land Between Tour' takes you to traditional villages in the New Territories. The Feng Shui tour explores this traditional concept *(see box, page 24)*.

Hong Kong Dolphinwatch Ltd., 1528 Star House, Tsim Sha Tsui (tel: 2984 1414) has a half-day eco-cruise to sight Hong Kong's threatened pink dolphins.

If you are interested in hiring a guide for a group or a personal guide, contact HKTB in Hong Kong. Contact CITS for guides in other South China destinations.

H

HEALTH AND MEDICAL CARE (see also EMERGENCIES)

There are no special health precautions to take in Hong Kong. No vaccinations are needed. Food is safe, even in roadside stalls, and you can safely drink the water, though most people prefer bottled water. Avoid eating locally caught shellfish and oysters, and never eat them raw; most restaurants use imported or farmed varieties. Be aware that outside major hotels, MSG (monosodium glutamate) is widely used.

Travelling into China requires a few extra precautions. You should not drink the tap water; drink only bottled water and use bottled water to brush your teeth. However, the thermos of hot water supplied in all hotel rooms is perfectly safe to drink. It is also wise not to eat raw food in China; choose fruit that can be peeled.

a bottle of drinking water	**Yat tchun sui**
I want to see a...	**Ngor yiu tai...**
doctor	**Yee sang**
dentist	**Nga yee**

During the hot, humid summer months, remember to limit exposure to thc sun. Wear a hat and use a sunscreen. Always carry a bottle of water, especially when hiking.

HOLIDAYS

Thanks to the convergence of British and Chinese traditions, Hong Kong celebrates 17 holidays a year. Though the banks close, most businesses carry on as usual. The only holiday on which Hong Kong really shuts down is the Lunar New Year. Chinese holidays are fixed according to the lunar calendar, so exact dates cannot always be given.

January 1	New Year's Day
January or February	Lunar New Year (3 days)
March or April	Easter (Good Friday, Easter Monday)
April	Ching Ming Festival
April or May	Buddha's Birthday
May 1	Labour Day
May or June	Tuen Ng (Dragon Boat) Festival
July 1 (or first weekday)	Establishment Day of the Special Administrative Region
September	The day following the mid-Autumn Festival
October 1	National Day
October	Chung Yeung Festival
December 25	Christmas Day
December 26	Boxing Day (day after Christmas)

L

LANGUAGE

The official languages of Hong Kong are English and Chinese. While Chinese can be called the world's most widely spoken language, it actually has innumerable dialects – people from Beijing can't understand a word that people from Hong Kong say; in fact they can't even understand what people from Shanghai say. What has bound the country together over thousands of years is the written language.

Each Chinese character represents an idea – a meaning, not a sound. There are about 50,000 characters; some 5,000 of these are in common use. Writing a single character may require from 1 to 33 strokes. Written Chinese is a subtle language – choice of one character over another can convey delicate shades of meaning. Handwriting style is also important – the Chinese consider calligraphy a serious art form. Chinese is traditionally written in columns, read from top to bottom and right to left. However, today you often see printed Chinese characters presented much like a European language.

Putonghua, or Mandarin, is China's official language and is gradually becoming the lingua franca all over mainland China. Cantonese is spoken in Hong Kong and South China. While Putonghua has only four tones, Cantonese uses up to nine different tonal inflections to distinguish otherwise identical syllables. This makes Cantonese an especially difficult language for foreigners to learn.

The following approximations of Cantonese greetings may help you make contact with the locals:

Good morning	**Jo sahn**
Good afternoon	**Ng on**
Good evening	**Mang on**
Good night	**Jo tow**
Goodbye	**Joy geen**
Please (for service)	**M goi**
Please (invitation)	**Ching**
Thank you (for service)	**M goi**
Thank you (for a gift)	**Daw jeh**

Here are some everyday Hong Kong words:

amah	housemaid
chop	seal or stamp on a document
fung shui	lucky siting of building or graves
gwailo	Europeans, foreigners
hong	big business firm
joss	luck
yam seng	'cheers', 'bottoms up'

Getting around is difficult when place names are pronounced differently in English and Cantonese. Kowloon (Nine Dragons) sounds similar in both languages; here are some that differ:

Aberdeen	**Heung Gong Jai**
Causeway Bay	**Tung Lo Wan**
Central District	**Jung Wan**
Cross Harbour Tunnel	**Hoi Dai Sui Do**
Happy Valley	**Pau Ma Dei**
Ocean Park	**Hoi Yeung Gung Yuen**
The Peak	**San Deng**
Peak Tram	**Lam Che**
Repulse Bay	**Chin Sui Wan**
Stanley	**Chek Chue**
Star Ferry Pier	**Tin Sing Ma Tau**

M

MEDIA

Newspapers and Magazines. Local English-language dailies are the *South China Morning Post* and the *Hong Kong Standard;* the

China Daily is a Hong Kong-published version of China's national English-language daily. The *Asian Wall Street Journal,* published Monday–Friday in Hong Kong, focuses on business and financial affairs. The *International Herald Tribune,* edited in Paris, is printed simultaneously in Hong Kong six days a week. Newspapers and magazines from Europe, Asia and the US are easily available at hotels and bookshops.

Radio and Television. Hong Kong has two TV channels in English and two in Chinese. The Chinese channels sometimes show foreign-language films which are dubbed into Cantonese; satellite and cable stations are also available. The 'Star World' satellite station shows re-runs of US and British television programmes.

There are six English-language radio channels providing a broad range, from easy listening to news and current affairs. The BBC World Service also broadcasts 24 hours a day at 675 kHz.

MONEY

Currency. Hong Kong's currency is freely convertible, and is pegged to the US dollar at a rate of around 7.8. The Hong Kong dollar is divided into 100 cents. Banknotes are circulated in denominations of HK$10, HK$20, HK$50, HK$100, HK$500 and HK$1,000. Banknotes are issued by three local banks, Hongkong and Shanghai Banking Corporation, the Bank of China and the Standard Chartered Bank. Coins, however, are minted by the Hong Kong government; they come in denominations of 10, 20 and 50 cents and HK$1, HK$2, HK$5 and HK$10. Note that the 10-cent and 50-cent pieces look confusingly alike. Britain's Queen Elizabeth, who once appeared on these coins, has been replaced by the flower of the bauhinia tree, Hong Kong's regional emblem.

Currency in Macau and China. In China, the *renminbi* (RMB) or *yuan* is not a fully convertible currency; you can change your Hong Kong dollars (or any other currency) to *yuan* in China but you are only allowed to change *yuan* back to foreign currency provided you have a receipt of the original transaction. However, Hong Kong dollars are accepted in both Guangzhou and Shenzhen. Macau's currency is the *pataca*, and the same rules apply. Both the *yuan* and the *pataca* have an exchange value roughly the equivalent of the Hong Kong dollar, i.e. you will be charged in Hong Kong dollars about what you would be charged if you were paying in *patacas* or *yuan*.

Currency Exchange. Foreign currencies can be exchanged at banks, hotels, money changers and major shopping outlets. Banks have better exchange rates, but charge a commission. Licensed money changers charge no commission, but the rates offered are about equivalent to a 5 percent commission. Money changers are found in all tourist areas and are open on holidays and late into the evening.

ATMs. ATMs are found all over Hong Kong, and banks do not usually charge a fee for the service. There are ATMs in Guangzhou and Shenzhen, but these are harder to find.

Credit Cards. Credit cards and charge cards are accepted everywhere you go in Hong Kong. Major hotels, restaurants and shops in China also accept the well-known credit cards.

Traveller's Cheques. Traveller's cheques are widely accepted in shops, though you'll probably get a better exchange rate at a bank. You must show your passport when you cash a cheque. They are particularly useful in China, where you may not find an ATM.

O

OPENING HOURS

Most government offices are open 9am–1pm and 2–5pm Monday–Friday, and 9am–1pm Saturday.

Banking hours are usually 9am–4.30pm Monday–Friday, and 9am–12.30pm Saturday. Some banks stop transactions an hour before closing time.

Business offices are normally open Monday–Friday 9am–5pm, closed for lunch 1–2pm; Saturday 9am–5pm. Most post offices are open Monday–Friday 9.30am–5pm and Saturday until 1pm.

Most shops are open seven days a week. Shops on Hong Kong Island are open 10am–7pm in Central, 10am–9.30 pm in Wan Chai, and 10am–10pm or later in Causeway Bay and Tsim Sha Tsui.

Museums are open from 10 or 11am–6pm. Most close one day a week, and some close on public holidays.

P

POLICE

The Hong Kong Police Force is one of the world's best equipped, with computerised and radio-controlled operations. The police deal not only with crime and traffic but also coast guard duties. Living up to Hong Kong's reputation as a fashion centre, they dress in smart, tailored uniforms. Most police can speak some English.

Where's the police station, please?	**Chai goon haih been do a, m goi?**

POST OFFICES

The main post office is on Hong Kong Island at 2 Connaught Place, just to the west of the Star Ferry terminal. There is a philatelic center on the ground floor; mailing and stamps are taken care of on the first floor. In Kowloon, post offices are located at 405 Nathan Road, between the Jordan and Yau Ma Tei underground stations, and at 10 Middle Road, one block north of Salisbury Road. For information, tel: 2921 2222.

Post offices in Hong Kong deal only with mailing letters and packages. For faxing, telex and other services, see the business centre in your hotel.

PUBLIC TRANSPORT

Hong Kong's public transport system is one of the most efficient and easy to use anywhere; it's also remarkably inexpensive. Be aware that buses, ferries, and trams require the exact fare, so it is wise to carry some small change. The Octopus Card, which can be purchased at MTR stations, is a convenient electronic card accepted on most buses and ferries, the MTR system, trams, trains in the New Territories, and the Airport Express Line. It costs HK$150 (including an HK$50 refundable deposit), and can be reloaded in units of HK$50 or HK$100 at MTR stations or convenience stores.

MTR. Hong Kong's Mass Transit Railway is one of the world's most modern, attractive, and easy-to-use undergrounds. It operates daily 6am–1am, and connects Kowloon, Hong Kong Island and the New Territories. The five lines are colour-coded; signs and announcements are in both English and Cantonese. Tickets for single fares, ranging from HK$4–HK$26 depending on distance, can be purchased from vending machines. Be sure to take your ticket when it pops up on the turnstile; you will need it to exit when you reach your destination.

Ferries. The Star Ferry is not just a means of transportation, but a not-to-be missed visitor experience. The ferry connects Tsim Sha Tsui with Hong Kong Island at Central, and runs daily 6.30am–11.30pm every three to five minutes, and costs HK$1.70 for ordinary class and HK$2.20 for first class on the upper deck. Passengers aged 65 or above (upon production of HKID or senior citizen card) go free.

There are many other ferries connecting sections of the city: from Central to Hung Hom; from Wan Chai to Tsim Sha Tsui and Hung Hom; and the hoverferry service between Central and Tsim Sha Tsui East (near Hung Hom KCR Railway Station).

Ferries to the outlying islands are operated by New World First Ferry (for Lantau, Cheung Chau and Peng Chau, tel: 2131 8181) and Hong Kong and Kowloon Ferry (for Lamma, tel: 2815 6063). All depart from the Outlying Island Ferry Piers west of the Star Ferry terminus on Central. Fares vary, with the highest being

HK$27. Jetfoils and catamarans to Macau leave from the Macau Ferry Terminal, just west of the Star Ferry about every 15 minutes 7am–5.30pm and every hour 6pm–6am; one-way fares are HK$130–HK$247, slightly more at the weekend.

Buses. The bus service in Hong Kong is good and relatively cheap. Double-decker buses run 24 hours (night bus numbers are prefixed by an 'N') and cover even remote parts of Hong Kong. Fares range from HK$1.20–HK$45, depending on distance, and the exact fare must be put in the box next to the driver as you get on. There are three bus companies: New World First Bus (tel: 2136 8888), Kowloon Motor Bus (KMB, tel: 2745 4466) and Citybus (tel: 2873 0818). Major bus terminals are located on both sides of the Star Ferry, and on Hong Kong Island at Exchange Square.

'Public Light Buses' seat 16 passengers. You can hail them everywhere and get off almost anywhere along their route. Tell the driver when you want to get off and pay as you leave. Minibuses marked with a green stripe go to the Mid Levels, up to the Peak and to Aberdeen. You can find them in Central and along Nathan Road. Minibuses are red and yellow, and you generally pay when you get off. Maxicabs are distinctive green-and-yellow vans that run set routes and you pay as you get on. The fares for both range from HK$2-HK$22.50. Destinations are marked by a sign in English and Chinese on the front, but the English is often smaller and hard to read. Both ply routes around Hong Kong Island, and in Kowloon, while a few carry passengers between the two.

Trams. Hong Kong's picturesque double-decker trams are also a tourist attraction and provide a pleasant way to see the sights. Slow but sure, they traverse the north coast of Hong Kong Island between Kennedy Town and Shau Kei Wan. Pick one up on Des Voeux, Queensway, or Hennessy roads. Enter at the rear and exit at the front, dropping HK$2 into the fare box as you leave. It's a flat rate regardless of the distance travelled. The service operates between 6am and 1am.

Trains. The Kowloon-Canton Railway (KCR) runs 34km (21 miles) from Hung Hom in Kowloon to the border of China, and the local trains that serve commuters in the New Territories are an excellent way of visiting some of the towns and villages of the New Territories. Generally trains run daily every 3–10 minutes. Fares are very reasonable, costing HK$9 for standard class from Hung Hom to Sheung Shui and HK$18 for first class.

There is also a Light Rail Transit system (LRT) that operates in the northwestern part of the New Territories linking the towns of Tuen Mun and Yuen Long. Trains run from 5.30am until 12.30am during the week and 6am–midnight on Sundays and public holidays.

Taxis. Hong Kong's metered taxis can be hailed on the street. Taxis on Hong Kong Island and Kowloon are red. Fares start at HK$15 for the first 2km (1.2 miles), and go up HK$1.40 for every 200m; there are extra charges for luggage (HK$5 per piece) and trips through tunnels (HK$20 for the Cross-Harbour Tunnel). Be warned that taxi drivers often don't speak English, so it's a good idea to have your destination and the name of your hotel written in Chinese. Many hotels print a list of well-known places in Chinese characters and English that you can carry with you to show to your driver.

Funicular. The modernised Peak Tram funicular railway links Garden Road with Victoria Peak. The climb straight up the mountainside to the Peak Tower takes a breathtaking eight minutes; from the top there's a panoramic view. The tram costs HK$20 and runs daily 7am–midnight every 10 minutes or so.

R

RELIGION

Confucianism, Buddhism and Taoism or a mixture thereof are the major religions in Hong Kong. There are also Christian churches of every denomination, Islamic mosques, Hindu temples and Jewish and Baha'i houses of worship.

Visitors will find Anglican/Episcopal services at St John's Cathedral in Central on Hong Kong Island, and at St Andrew's Church on Nathan Road in Kowloon. Catholic masses are held at Rosary Chapel on South Chatham Road in Kowloon. For information about services, see the Saturday issue of the *South China Morning Post*, which carries announcements from churches.

Kowloon Mosque (Jamia Masjid) catering to Hong Kong's sizable Muslim population is beside Kowloon Park, on Nathan Road.

T

TELEPHONE

Hong Kong's country code is 852; Macau's country code is 853. Hong Kong has 8-digit numbers, while Macau's run to six figures. The telephone system in Hong Kong is excellent for both local and international calls, and you can expect a clear connection.

Subscribers in Hong Kong pay a flat fee, and are not charged for local calls, so if you want to make a local call, you can walk into any shop and ask to use the phone. Some shops keep their phone on the front counter. Public phones require a HK$1 coin or a phone card. Phone cards, available at 7-Eleven stores and Hong Kong Telephone's retail shops, have values of HK$25, HK$50 and HK$100. Hotels usually add a surcharge on both local and international calls.

For an English-speaking information service dial 1081; if you have difficulty in getting a number, dial 109. International direct-dial calls can be made at Hong Kong Telecom International, Shop 116, Princes Building, Des Voeux Road, Central. For overseas calls dial 001 (10011 for collect/reverse charge calls).

TIME DIFFERENCES

Before you make any overseas telephone calls, have a look at the following chart, so you won't wake someone halfway round the world. The hours refer to the months when many countries in the northern hemisphere move their clocks one hour ahead (Daylight Savings Time). Hong Kong stays the same year-round, at GMT + 8.

New York	London	**Hong Kong**	Sydney	Auckland
7am	noon	7pm	9pm	11pm

TIPPING

Tipping in Hong Kong is somewhat confusing; tipping was never customary in China, although the British introduced it to Hong Kong. Who should be tipped and when is not always clear, especially inside China. Most hotels and restaurants routinely add a 10 percent service charge, but in upmarket establishments, an extra 5–10 percent may be expected; in inexpensive places, round up the bill or leave up to 5 percent.

Unlike in Europe, tourist guides do not indicate that they expect a tip; however, they should receive about 10 percent of the cost of the tour. A hotel porter should receive HK$5–HK$10 per bag; an airport porter about HK$2. Hotel room attendants should get about 2 percent of the bill, but this is not obligatory. Lavatory attendents expect HK$2–HK$5, depending on the establishment. Tip hairdressers/barbers 10–15 percent. Tipping taxi and limo drivers is optional; you can simply round up the fare.

The best rule is to tip according to how you feel about the situation; anything you give will be graciously received.

TOILETS

Toilets are not easy to find in Hong Kong. The best bets are shopping malls, hotels,and restaurants where you have eaten a meal or snack, or fast food places. Places frequented by tourists and upmarket establishments will have Western toilets, both in Hong Kong, Guangzhou and on the islands. But you can encounter Chinese toilets in non-tourist areas or even in restaurants with a largely

Chinese clientele; most of these in Hong Kong are clean and well-maintained. Toilet paper is not always provided, so it is wise to carry your own. To use the Chinese toilet, face the hood; be sure you put your used toilet paper in the wastebasket.

Where are the toilets?	**Chi saw haih been do a?**

TOURIST INFORMATION

The Hong Kong Tourism Board (HKTB) operates information and gift centres at key areas for visitors; the first one you'll encounter is the counter in the arrival hall at Chek Lap Kok, open daily 7am–11pm. The main office is at The Center, 99 Queens Road in Central, open daily 8am–6pm. On the Kowloon side in Tsim Sha Tsui, an office is on the Star Ferry Concourse, open the same hours. The HKTB Visitor Hotline, tel: 2508 1234, operates daily 8am–6pm.

The HKTB publishes free brochures and literature about various aspects of Hong Kong; the *Official Hong Kong Guide* is a monthly information booklet with an overview of Hong Kong's attractions, shopping tips and current events and exhibitions. Free maps are available. Several weekly and monthly publications, free at restaurants and other outlets, tell you what's going on. *Hong Kong Diary* is a weekly publication; others are *BC* magazine and the *HK magazine*, both free from many bars, restaurants and bookshops. The *South China Morning Post* carries reviews and listings in its features section. The monthly publication, *Where,* free at HKTB offices, tells you what's going on in Hong Kong. The *South China Morning Post* has an entertainment section Friday.

There is also a counter for the Macau Government Tourist Office (MGTO) (tel: 2769 7970) at Chek Lap Kok, open daily 9am–10.30pm (closed for lunch and dinner). MGTO offices are at both ends of the Macau ferry terminal: Room 336, 3/F, on the departure floor in Hong Kong, and in the arrival hall at the Macau

Ferry Terminal. Maps of Macau are available as well as the publication *Macau Travel Talk* and the pamphlet *Macau Walking Tours*.

Overseas you can contact HKTB branch offices. Australia: Hong Kong House, Level 4, 80 Druitt Street, Sydney, NSW 2000, tel: (02) 9283 3083. Canada: Hong Kong Trade Centre, 9 Temperance Street, Toronto, Ontario M5H 1Y6, tel: (416) 366 2389. UK: 6 Grafton Street. London WIX 3LB, tel: (020) 7533 7100. US: 115 E. 54th Street, New York, NY 10022, tel: (212) 421 3382; 10940 Wilshire Boulevard, Suite 2050, Los Angeles CA 90024, tel: (310) 208 0233.

TRAVELLERS WITH DISABILITIES

Hong Kong is not an easy place for travellers with disabilities. Hong Kong's frequent steps and its many steep streets, narrow crowded footpaths and the pedestrian overpasses on Hong Kong Island are not easily negotiated. However, some hotels have special facilities for the disabled, most buildings have lifts, escalators are common, and taxis are inexpensive and easy to find. Contact HKTB for information on accommodation and advice on services catering to visitors with special needs. The Society for Advancement of Travel for the Handicapped (SATH) has a website <www.sath.org>.

W

WEBSITES

HKTB's website is <www.discoverhongkong.com>. The *South China Morning Post* has a site, <www.scmp.com.hk>. The website for the Hong Kong Arts Festival, which takes place in February, is <www.artsfestival.org>. Macau's tourist information website is <www.macautourism.gov.mo>. An excellent site for finding the best deal on air fares and booking flights and hotel accommodation is <www.travelocity.com>. For airfares try <www.bestfares.com>.

Many hotels offer internet access. If yours doesn't, there are cybercafés all over Hong Kong. Pacific Coffee Company is on

1/F, International Finance Centre, 1 Harbour View Street (tel: 2868 5100); i-Cable Station, 2/F is in Ocean Terminal, Harbour City, Tsim Sha Tsui.

The UK government has a useful website on health advice for travellers including updates on the latest warnings around the world at <www.doh.gov.uk/traveladvice/>.

WEIGHTS AND MEASURES

The international metric system is in official use. However, Chinese measurements are still commonly used.

Food products are generally sold by the *catty* (1.3lbs/600g). Other items are measured by the *tael* (1.3oz/38g), and the *chin* (1.10lb/300 g). For length, the *tsün* (1.5in/37mm) and *check* (1.2ft/37cm) are used in markets.

Y

YOUTH HOSTELS

Hong Kong's youth hostels are located in remote scenic areas, but are easily accessible by public transport. The main hostels are Jockey Club Mount Davis Youth Hostel, top of Mt Davis Path, Mt. Davis, Western District (tel: 2817 5715); and Bradbury Lodge, 66 Ting Kok Road, Tai Mei Tuk Tai Po, New Territories (tel: 2662 5123). For information, contact the Youth Hostels Association, tel: 2788 1638.

More centrally located budget establishments with simple or bunk-bed rooms include the BP International House, 8 Austin Road, Tsim Sha Tsui (tel: 2376 1111); Booth Lodge, run by the Salvation Army, 11 Wing Sing Lane, Yau Ma Tei (tel: 2771 9266; <www.boothlodge.salvation.org.hk/>); and the YWCA's Garden View International House, overlooking the Zoo at 1 MacDonnell Road, Central (tel: 2877 3737; <www.ywca.org.hk/hotel/Eng/home2.htm>).

Recommended Hotels

Hong Kong has some of the most luxurious hotels in the world, with representatives from all the major international chains. Hotels listed below have full air-conditioning, offer 24-hour or limited room service, and a wide range of facilities. Hong Kong hotels have excellent business services and conference facilities; many have shopping malls.

Reservations are strongly recommended, particularly in summer and at Christmas. If you do arrive without making advance arrangements, the Hong Kong Hotel Reservation Centre at the International Airport will be happy to arrange accommodation for you on your arrival.

As a basic guide, the symbols below have been used to indicate high-season rates in Hong Kong dollars, based on double occupancy, with bath or shower. Unless otherwise noted, hotels take all major credit cards. A 10 percent service charge and 3 percent government tax will be added to the bill.

$$$$	above HK$2,500
$$$	HK$I,600 to HK$2,500
$$	HK$950 to HK$1,600
$	below HK$950

CENTRAL

Conrad International Hong Kong $$$$ *Pacific Place, 88 Queensway, tel: 2521 3838, fax: 2521 3888; <www.conrad.com. hk>.* A modern hotel set above Pacific Place with good views over the city. Rooms have classic furnishings with wood panelling and polished granite; all have voice mail, fax machines and dataports. Nicolini's is a fine Italian restaurant; there are also Cantonese, French and international restaurants. Business centre and conference facilities, health centre, outdoor swimming pool. 513 rooms.

Island Shangri-La Hong Kong $$$$ *Pacific Place, Supreme Court Road, tel: 2877 3838, fax: 2521 8742; <www.shangri-la.*

com>. The outstanding feature here is a 17-storey atrium with abundant greenery. Large rooms with oversize bathrooms have dataports and views of the harbour or Victoria Peak. Continental, Cantonese and Japanese restaurants. Conference facilities and business centre, outdoor swimming pool and a 24-hour gym. 565 rooms.

Mandarin Oriental $$$$ *5 Connaught Road, tel: 2522 0111, fax: 2810 6190; <www.mandarin-oriental.com>*. Located in the heart of the business district, this landmark hotel is rated as one of the top hotels of the world. Most of the spacious rooms have balconies and views over the harbour. Restaurants include the trendy Vong as well as international food. Conference facilities, translation service, indoor swimming pool, fitness centre and beauty salon. 541 rooms.

CAUSEWAY BAY/WAN CHAI

Empire Hotel $$ *33 Hennessy Road, Wan Chai, tel: 2866 9111, fax: 2861 3121; <www.asiastandard.com/hotel/empirehk.html>*. A good value hotel in the heart of Wan Chai, it has many of the services and facilities of higher-priced hotels. Rooms are comfortable and pleasant with many amenities. Cantonese, a recommended Shanghainese restaurant and a wine bar. Business and conference centre, health centre, swimming pool. 345 rooms.

The Excelsior $$$ *281 Gloucester Road, Causeway Bay, tel: 2894 8888, fax: 2895 6459; <www.mandarin-oriental.com>*. This hotel is located near Victoria Park, and hosts many tour groups. Guest rooms are spacious, and have views over the bay or park. Cantonese and European restaurants and an English-style pub with live entertainment. Business centre, rooftop tennis courts, fitness room and Jacuzzi. 884 rooms.

Grand Hyatt Hong Kong $$$$ *1 Harbour Road, Wan Chai, tel: 2588 1234, fax: 2802 0677; <www.hongkong.grand.hyatt.com>*. A futuristic design of marble and glass, magnificent views over Hong Kong harbour, and an art-deco style interior characterise Hyatt International's Asian flagship hotel. It hosted President

Clinton during his 1998 visit. Rooms are smart and contemporary with luxurious amenities. Three restaurants, including Milanese and Cantonese cuisine, and JJ's, a hot nightspot. Business centre, reference library, private boardroom, outdoor swimming pool, gym, tennis courts, golf driving range, jogging track. 556 rooms.

Novotel Century Hong Kong $$ *238 Jaffe Road, tel: 2598 8888, fax: 2598 8866.* This 23-storey hotel is a short walk via covered walkway to the Convention and Exhibition Centre. Rooms are small, but equipped with double-glazed windows to shut out traffic noise. Business centre, conference rooms, outdoor swimming pool, health centre, putting green and an Italian restaurant. 516 rooms.

Park Lane $$$ *310 Gloucester Road, Causeway Bay, tel: 2293 8888, fax: 2576 7853; <www.parklane.com.hk>.* Across from Victoria Park, this attractive hotel with modern marble décor is near to restaurants, shops and department stores. Room prices vary by floor. Top floor restaurant serves international cuisine with an Asian influence, and Stix is a bar/American restaurant/nightclub. Conference facilities and business centre, health centre, beauty salon. 792 rooms.

Renaissance Harbour View $$$ *1 Harbour Road, Wan Chai, tel: 2802 8888, fax: 2802 8833; <www.renaissancehotels.com>.* This spectacular hotel adjoins the Convention and Exhibition Centre on the Wan Chai waterfront. About half of the rooms have harbour views, and all are equipped with faxes and voice mail. The hotel's outdoor swimming pool is one of the largest in Hong Kong. Cantonese, Continental and international restaurants. Business centre and conference facilities, fitness centre, beauty salon, rooftop tennis court, jogging track, garden, swimming pool and nightclub. 860 rooms.

Wharney Hotel $$ *61-73 Lockhart Road, Wan Chai, tel: 2861 1000; 2529 5133; <www.wharney.com>.* This pleasant hotel offers small but comfortable rooms; those with views are most expensive. Cantonese restaurant, Western/Asian buffet, bar with live entertainment. Business centre, outdoor swimming pool and whirlpool, fitness centre. 358 rooms.

KOWLOON

Holiday Inn Golden Mile $$$ *50 Nathan Road, Tsim Sha Tsui, tel: 2369 3111, fax: 2369 8016; <wwwgoldenmile.com>*. This hotel is conveniently located in the midst of Nathan Road's 'Golden Mile' shopping. Rooms are a good size and modern with floor-to-ceiling windows, although views are blocked by nearby buildings. Fine restaurants including German and Cantonese cuisine. Business centre, rooftop swimming pool, health centre and sauna. 600 rooms.

Intercontinental Grand Stanford Hotel $$$ *70 Mody Road, Tsim Sha Tsui East, tel: 2721 5161, fax: 2732 2233; <www.hongkong.intercontinental.com>*. On the waterfront, with views over the harbour, this recently renovated hotel near the Coliseum has hosted the likes of David Bowie and Elton John. About half the rooms have harbour views. French, Italian and Cantonese restaurants. Business centre, heated outdoor pool and gym. Free shuttle service in Tsim Sha Tsui. 579 rooms.

Kowloon Hotel $$$ *19–21 Nathan Road, Tsim Sha Tsui, tel: 2929 2888, fax: 2739 9811; <www.fasttrack.kowloon.peninsula.com>*. A high-tech glass-and-steel hotel just behind the Peninsula and under the same management, this is an especially pleasant and convenient hotel for the business traveller. Rooms are small but attractive and cosy, and equipped with fax and computer with free internet access and e-mail. Cantonese and Italian restaurants, and Western/Asian buffet. Business centre, beauty salon and tour desk. 736 rooms.

Kowloon Shangri La $$$ *64 Mody Road, Tsim Sha Tsui East, tel: 2721 2111, fax: 2723 8686; <www.shangri-la.com>* Relaxed atmosphere and good service. Rooms are large and luxurious with dataports and all amenities; some have harbour views. Napa, on the 21st floor, offers Californian cuisine and a great view; there is also French, Cantonese and Japanese cuisine, business centre, indoor swimming pool, health spa and beauty salon. 725 rooms.

Majestic Hotel $ *348 Nathan Road, Yau Ma Tei, tel: 2781 1333, fax: 2781 1773; <www.majestichotel.com.hk>*. Located in a complex on upper Nathan Road, this hotel offers plain but comfortable, contemporary rooms. There is only a coffee shop, but the complex has shops, a cinema and lots of restaurants. 380 rooms.

Marco Polo Gateway $$$ *Harbour City, 3 Canton Road, Tsim Sha Tsui, tel: 2113 0888, fax: 2113 0022; <www.marcopolohotels.com>.* One of a trio of Marco Polo hotels, it's located in the Harbour City shopping complex, a step from the Star Ferry terminal; others are the higher-priced Hong Kong Hotel and the newly renovated Prince. It's a good choice for business travellers, with large desks and voice mail in all of its good-size rooms. One French restaurant, but Harbour City restaurants are nearby. Business centre and conference facilities. 431 rooms.

Miramar Hotel $$ *118–130 Nathan Road, Tsim Sha Tsui;Tel: 2368 111, fax: 2369 1788; <www.miramarhk.com>.* This relaxed and friendly hotel has a great location overloooking Kowloon Park with a five-minute walk from the bars and restaurants of Tsim Sha Tsui. Chinese and fusion food and a slightly tacky nightclub. Fitness centre, indoor swimming pool and sauna. 525 rooms.

Nathan Hotel $ *378 Nathan Road, Yau Ma Tei, tel: 2388 5141, fax: 2770 4262; <www.nathanhotel.com>.* Recently renovated, this quiet and pleasant hotel near the Temple Street Night Market has spacious, nicely decorated no-frills rooms. The Penthouse restaurant serves Cantonese and Western food. Business centre. 185 rooms.

Park Hotel $$ *61–65 Chatham Road South, Tsim Sha Tsui, tel: 2366-1371, fax: 2739-7259; <www.parkhotel.com.hk>.* This is one of the best hotels in the moderate category, located across from the Science Museum. The lobby is attractive, and rooms are large and well-furnished. Western and Cantonese restaurants plus coffee and cake shop. Conference rooms and business services. 430 rooms.

Peninsula $$$$ *Salisbury Road, Tsim Sha Tsui, tel: 2920 2888, fax: 2722 4170; <www.fasttrack.hongkong.peninsula.com>.* Hong Kong's most historic hotel, first opened in 1928, is a study in colonial elegance. The famous English-style afternoon tea in the lobby is a must for visitors. Guest rooms in the new 32-storey tower offer spectacular views; furnishings and amenities are sumptuous, and service is of the highest standard. Gaddi's is Hong Kong's premier French restaurant; other fine choices offer Pacific Rim, continental, Swiss, Japanese and Cantonese cuisine. Business centre, fax in all rooms, beauty salon, spa facilities, health club, swimming pool with sun terrace, music room. 300 rooms.

InterContinental Hong Kong $$$$ *18 Salisbury Road, Kowloon, tel: 2721 1211, fax: 2739 4546; <hongkongic.china.intercontinental.com/index.shtml>*. One of Hong Kong's top hotels, set on the waterfront, with luxurious granite and marble décor and harbour views. Guest rooms have spacious Italian marble bathrooms. Service is excellent and the hotel has some of Hong Kong's best restaurants. Business centre, outdoor swimming pool, health spa, exercise room. 606 rooms.

Royal Garden $$$–$$$$ *69 Mody Road, Tsim Sha Tsui East, tel: 2721 5215, fax: 2369 9976; <www.rghk.com.hk>*. This is one of Hong Kong's most attractive hotels. All rooms open onto terraces overlooking a plant-filled 15-storey atrium with pools and waterfalls. Rooms are cosy and inviting; the most expensive have harbour views. Italian, Cantonese and Japanese restaurants and a restaurant in the atrium. Business centre, rooftop swimming pool and Jacuzzi, sports centre, beauty salon, fitness room, putting green. 422 rooms.

Royal Pacific Hotel and Towers $$–$$$ *33 Canton Road, Tsim Sha Tsui, tel: 2736 1188, fax: 2736 1212; <www.royalpacific.com.hk>*. This is actually two hotels, located across from Kowloon Park and surrounded by greenery. The Royal Pacific is the more moderately priced. Its rooms are attractive but rather small. The Towers is more upmarket, with harbour views from the highest rooms. The hotels share facilities. One restaurant, business centre, fitness room and squash courts. 673 rooms.

Salisbury YMCA $ *41 Salisbury Road, Tsim Sha Tsui, tel: 2268 7000, fax: 2739 9315; <www.ymcahk.org.hk>*. Reserve well in advance for this hotel, located next door to the Peninsula. It's one of the best bargains in Hong Kong, offering the facilities and service of much more expensive hotels at a fraction of the cost. Rooms are simple in décor, but comfortable and well-equipped. Restaurant and food outlets. Two swimming pools, fitness gym and sports centre with squash courts and climbing wall. 380 units.

Shamrock $ *223 Nathan Road, Yau Ma Tei; Kowloon, tel: 2735 2271, fax: 2736 7354; <www.shamrockhotel.com.hk>*. In a rather plain modern building, the hotel has a lobby decorated with chandeliers and artwork. Guest rooms are small but clean (cheaper rooms are without windows). 158 rooms.

Sheraton Hong Kong Hotel and Towers $$$$ *20 Nathan Road, Tsim Sha Tsui, tel: 2369 1111, fax: 2739 8707; <www.sheraton.com/hongkong>*. Located near the harbourfront, across from the Hong Kong Space Museum and the Hong Kong Art Museum. The décor is contemporary with Asian motifs. Guest rooms facing the harbour have great views. Restaurants include Japanese, an oyster bar and Mexican. Business centre and conference facilities, rooftop pool and Jacuzzi, sauna and gym. 780 rooms.

NEW TERRITORIES

Silvermine Beach Hotel $–$$ *Silvermine Bay, Mui O, Lantau, tel: 2984 8295, Fax: 2984 1907; <www.resort.com.hk/h0201.htm>*. A pleasant if basic hotel overlooking Silvermine Bay on Lantau Island, a half-hour ferry-ride from Central, and convenient for buses to fine beaches, country walks and the Big Buddha. Coffee shop and Chinese restaurant. The beach here is a bit polluted, but the hotel has an outdoor swimming pool, gym, sauna and tennis courts. 128 rooms.

Royal Park $$ *8 Pak Hok Ting Street, Sha Tin, tel: 2601 2111, fax: 2601 366; <www.royalpark.com.hk>*. This hotel near Sha Tin's New Town Plaza shopping complex is easily accessed from the city by KCR or the hotel's shuttle bus to Tsim Sha Tsui. Chiu Chow and Japanese restaurants, coffee shop, squash, tennis and jogging facilities, swimming pool, health centre, business centre and conference facilities. Special facilities for guests with disabilities. 436 rooms.

MACAU

Lisboa $$ *Av. de Lisboa, No. 2–4, Macau, tel: (853) 377666, fax: 567193; <www.hotelisboa.com>.* This huge hotel on the waterfront with its cylindrical tower can't be missed. It has every facility, including casinos, a nightclub and show entertainment. Chinese, Portuguese, Continental and Asian restaurants. Conference and secretarial services, children's centre, outdoor swimming pool, fitness centre and free shuttle bus service. Around 1,000 rooms.

Posada de Sâo Tiago $$$ *Fortaleza de S. Tiago da Barrra, Av. da República, tel: (853) 378111, fax: 552170; <www.saotiago.com.mo>.* This charming small inn is built around the ruins of a fort dating from 1629. Guests here are treated with true Portuguese hospitality. Rooms are in Portuguese style with furniture imported from Portugal and blue-glazed tiles; most have balconies. Macanese cusine at Os Gatos, classic Portuguese cuisine at Café Da Barra. Outdoor swimming pool. 24 rooms.

GUANGZHOU (CANTON)

Garden Hotel $$ *368 Huanshi Dong Lu, tel: (020)8333 8989, fax: 8335 0467; <www.gardenhotel-guangzhou.com>.* This hotel is well-named for its beautiful gardens. It is located in upmarket northern Guangzhou, and has a spectacular lobby with a huge unsupported ceiling. Standard rooms have all amenities but a somewhat plain décor. Restaurants offer Western and Asian cuisine. Business services, swimming pool, tennis court, health club and dance club. 1,112 rooms.

White Swan $$$ *1 South Shamian Street, tel: (020)8188 6968, fax: 8186 1188; <www.whiteswanhotel.com>.* This luxury hotel is sited on historic Shamian Island beside the Pearl River. A spectacular décor includes a lobby with a cascading waterfall, and rooms are furnished with reproduction Chinese antiques. Cantonese, Beijing, Sichuan, Shanghai and Japanese cuisine. Business services, two swimming pools, health club, driving range, tennis courts, dance club and cruises on the Pearl River. 843 rooms.

Recommended Restaurants

Dining is one of the great Hong Kong experiences. The city is crammed with all kinds of restaurants, specialising in every imaginable kind of cuisine. Kowloon has a particularly high concentration of restaurants. It is impossible to choose more than a few from the vast range of possibilities. As everywhere else, the restaurant scene is in a constant state of flux, so it's wise to call and make a reservation before you leave your hotel.

The price symbols below are intended as a guide only, and are based on a standard three-course meal (or Asian equivalent), in Hong Kong dollars. These prices do not cover alcoholic drinks or such notoriously expensive items as bird's nest or shark's fin soup.

$$$$	over HK$600 per person
$$$	HK$300 to HK$600 per person
$$	HK$150 to HK$300 per person
$	below HK$150 per person

KOWLOON

City Chiu Chow Restaurant $$ *1/F, East Ocean Centre, 98 Granville Road, Tsim Sha Tsui, tel: 2723 6226.* Open daily 11am to midnight. This large, bright restaurant overlooking a garden serves hearty Chiu Chow dishes and a variety of regional specialities. It features a big fish tank, and the shark's fin soup is more strongly flavoured than the Cantonese variety.

Fat Angelo's $–$$ *29-43 Ashley Road, Tsim Sha Tsui, tel: 2730 4788.* Open daily noon to midnight. A friendly uncomplicated American-Italian restaurant dishing up huge portions that can feed up to eight people. Children get an activity menu, but it also serves as a romantic setting with its checked tablecloths and wine served in tumblers. Other branches at 414 Jaffe Road, Causeway Bay and 49A-C Elgin Street, SoHo, Central.

Felix $$$$ *The Peninsula, Salisbury Road, tel: 2920 2888, ext 3188.* Open daily from 6pm, with last food orders at 10.30pm. This restaurant is not to be missed: the marvellous view and the striking Philippe Starck design are nearly as important as the food. The Pacific Rim fusion cuisine is delectable.

Great Shanghai $$ *26 Prat Avenue, Tsim Sha Tsui, tel: 2366 8158.* Open daily from 11am to midnight. Well-established restaurant serving good-value Shanghainese dishes. Beggar's Chicken is the house speciality (call in your order ahead). Typical warming dishes are Shanghainese dumplings, eel and bean curd dishes and cabbage stews. Shanghainese wines are also available. Friendly and helpful service.

Heichinrou Restaurant $$$ *2/F, Lippo Sun Plaza, 28 Canton Road, Tsim Sha Tsui, tel: 2375 7123.* Open daily from 11.30am to midnight. A chic Cantonese restaurant with stark modern décor. A good place for *dim sum.* Specialities include roasted pigeon with Chinese cheese sauce. There's a branch at the Times Square shopping centre in Causeway Bay.

Her Thai $$ *Shop 1, Promenade Level Tower 1, China Hong Kong City, 33 Canton Road, Tsim Sha Tsui, tel: 2735 8898.* Open daily noon to 11pm. Fabulous for its views of the harbour taking in the Central skyline. One of Hong Kong's most romantic settings with it gentle lighting and red hanging lanterns. Reasonably-priced and fine Thai food.

Jade Garden Restaurant $$ *Star House, 3 Salisbury Road, Tsim Sha Tsui, tel: 2730 6888.* Open daily Monday to Saturday 11am to 11pm and Sunday 10am to 11.30pm. Classic dishes, *dim sum* and seasonal specialities. Ask for the recommended dishes of the day.

Jimmy's Kitchen $$ *Kowloon Centre, 29 Ashley Road, Tsim Sha Tsui, tel: 2376 0327.* Open daily 11am to 11pm. One of Hong Kong's oldest restaurants, Jimmy's specialises in British food, but also has curries and other Asian dishes. There's also a Jimmy's in the South China Building, 1–3 Wyndham Street in Central.

Joyful Vegetarian $$ *530 Nathan Road, Yau Ma Tei, tel: 2780 2230.* Open 11am to 11pm. It is hard to find strictly vegetarian food in Hong Kong; most chefs add meat broth to vegetarian dishes. This restaurant is one of a handful that specialises in true vegetarian meals. Try the delicious country-style hotpot.

Pizzeria $$ *2/F Kowloon Hotel, 19–21 Nathan Road, Tsim Sha Tsui, tel: 2929 2888.* Open daily noon to 3pm and 6 to 11pm. Despite its name, this restaurant specialises in pasta, with a menu that changes often. The atmosphere is relaxed, and there's a wide range of choices of northern Italian dishes. Pizza is also on the menu.

Spice Market $$ *3/F, Marco Polo Prince Hotel, 23 Canton Road, Tsim Sha Tsui, tel: 2113 6046.* Open daily 6am to 12.30am. This pleasant restaurant specialises in a wide variety of Asian foods: Japanese, Chinese, Thai, Indian curries, hotpots, satays and more.

Tai Woo Restaurant $ *14–16 Hillwood Road, Tsim Sha Tsui, tel: 2368 5420.* Open until 3am. Popular favourites at this restaurant include seafood dishes such as steamed garoupa or sautéed scallops. The set meals are a good way of sampling a range of Cantonese dishes.

Yan Toh Heen $$$$ *InterContinental Hotel, 18 Salisbury Road, Tsim Sha Tsui, tel: 2721 1211.* Elegant restaurant with opulent décor and views over the harbour, serves exquisite and innovative Cantonese and Chinese food. The menu changes each lunar month.

CENTRAL

Ashoka Restaurant $ *G/F, 57–59 Wyndham Street, tel: 2524 9623.* Open daily noon to 2.30pm and 6 to 10.30pm. Elegant Indian restaurant serving delicately spiced northern Indian cuisine. The wide range of dishes offered includes tandoori, curries and vegetarian specialities. The place is small, so there may be a wait.

Beirut $$–$$$ *G/F-1/F, 27 D'Aguilar Street, Lan Kwai Fong, Central, tel: 2804 6611.* Open Monday to Thursday noon to 3pm,

6 to 11pm, Friday and Saturday, noon to 3pm, 6pm to midnight and Sunday 6 to 11pm. This restaurant offers an extensive menu of Lebanese specialities, including *shawarma* and *lahme bil agine* (a kind of Lebanese pizza). The homemade hummus is the best in Hong Kong. Ideal for lunch.

Habibi $$–$$ *112–114 Wellington Street, Central, tel: 2544 9298.* Open Monday to Thursday 11am to midnight and Friday and Saturday 11am to 2am, closed Sunday. Beautifully decorated with velvet seats, mirrors, niches with couches and hookah pipes. Great Egyptian food with a selection of hot and cold meze, including plenty of vegetarian choices. Weekend belly dancing.

Kiku Japanese Restaurant $$$ *1st Basement, Gloucester Tower, The Landmark, Des Voeux Road Central, tel: 2521 3344.* Open daily 11.30am to 3pm and 6 to 10.30pm. Traditional pine-panelled restaurant serving *teppanyaki* and *sushi* delicacies, *kaiseki*, or *sukiyaki* or *shabu-shabu* set meals. The *à la carte* menu features Kyoto-style cuisine; grilled codfish and eel are particularly recommended.

Luk Yu Tea House $$$ *24–26 Stanley Street, tel: 2523 1970.* Open daily 7am to 11pm (*dim sum* until 6pm). This place has been around for 60 years, and is a living piece of colonial history with its carved wooden doors and panelling. It is a popular venue for excellent *dim sum.*

M at the Fringe $$$$ *2 Lower Albert Road, Central, tel: 2877 4000.* Open Monday to Saturday noon to 2.30pm and 7 to 10.30pm, Sunday 7 to 10pm. Consistently voted one of Hong Kong's top restaurants. The fare is experimental Continental with amazing desserts. Dress smart, take a lot of money, and enjoy the elegant and relaxing atmosphere.

Ning Po Residents Association $$ *4/F Yip Fung Building, 10 D'Aguilar Street, Lan Kwai Fong, Central, tel: 2523 0648.* Open daily noon to 2.30pm and 6 to 10.30pm. Typical clattering canteen style restaurant hidden inside a commercial building. Its enormous range of Shanghai and Ningpo dishes come well recommended. A Hong Kong institution.

Peking Garden $$ *Shop 003, The Mall, Pacific Place, 88 Queensway, tel: 2845 8452.* Open daily 11.30am to 3pm and 5.30 to midnight. Lively restaurant specialising in northern Chinese dishes. Watch fresh noodles being made each evening, and enjoy the Peking Duck-carving exhibitions and Beggar's Chicken clay-breaking ceremonies. Other branches are at Star House, 3 Salisbury Road in Tsim Sha Tsui and at 500 Hennessy Road, Causeway Bay.

Vong $$$$ *Mandarin Oriental Hotel, 5 Connaught Road, tel: 2825 4028.* Open daily noon to 3pm and 6pm to midnight. A dramatic restaurant with a creative crossover cuisine of Asian flavours and French techniques. There are extensive vegetarian offerings. The tasting menu is recommended.

THE PEAK

Café Deco $$$ *1/F-2/F Peak Galleria, 118 Peak Road, tel: 2849 5111.* Open daily 10am to midnight. You won't find the greatest food here, but it has one of the best views in the city. There's a variety of Asian and Continental dishes, an oyster bar and live jazz at the weekend.

WAN CHAI

American Restaurant $ *Golden Star Building G/F-2/F, 20 Lockhart Road, tel: 2527 1000.* Open daily 11am to 11.30pm. Popular Peking restaurant (despite the name), featuring northern Chinese dishes, such as seafood noodles and the classic Peking duck. Speciality is a 'Four Great Happiness', a combination dish of pork, beef, prawns and chicken.

Cinta Restaurant $$ *1/F-2/F, Shing Yip Building, 10 Fenwick Street, tel: 2527 1199.* Open daily 11am to 5am. A friendly restaurant serving Indonesian favourites such as satay, prawn chili, fried squid and beef Rendang. Filipino dishes include crispy *pata* (pork leg) and mixed *adobo*. There are also Malaysian favourites. Live music nightly.

Fook Lam Moon $$$–$$$$ *35–45 Johnston Road, tel: 2866 0663.* Open daily 11.30am to 3pm and 6.30 to 11.30pm. One of the top Cantonese restaurants in the city. Seafood is the speciality, and here you can try shark's fin soup. There is also a branch at 53–59 Kimberler Road in Tsim Sha Tsui.

Viceroy $$–$$$ *2/F, Sun Hung Kai Centre, 30 Harbour Road, tel: 2827 7777.* Open daily noon to 3pm and 6 to 11pm. Indian restaurant with panoramic harbour views from an outdoor terrace, serving subtly flavoured tandoori, curry and vegetarian specialities, and an all-you-can-eat weekday buffet feast.

CAUSEWAY BAY

Cammino Restaurant $$ *I/F, The Excelsior, 281 Gloucester Road, Causeway Bay, tel: 2837 6780.* Open daily noon to 2.30pm and 6 to 11pm. Very popular Italian restaurant with an appetising menu of classic and modern dishes. Try the Spinosini pasta with lamb ragout and cherry tomatoes.

Kung Lak Tam $ *Lok Sing Centre, 31 Yee Wo Street, tel: 2890 3127.* Open daily 11am to 11pm. This Shanghainese vegetarian restaurant uses only the freshest produce, no MSG. The vegetable soup and fried noodles are especially delectable.

Padang $$ *JP Plaza, 22-26 Paterson Street, tel: 2881 5075.* Open daily 11am–11pm. Causeway Bay is the centre for Indonesian workers in the territory. The traditionally-clad staff are helpful, and serve delicious Indonesian staples from *nasi goreng* to *rembang padang*.

Red Pepper $$$ *7 Lan Fong Road, tel: 2577 3811.* Open daily 11.30am to 11.15pm. The right place for those who like spicy food. Sichuan-style cuisine in a friendly, relaxed atmosphere. The staff will help you to order a meal that suits your taste.

ABERDEEN

Aberdeen Jumbo Floating Restaurant $$–$$$ *Aberdeen Harbour, tel: 2553 9111.* Open daily 10.30am to 11.30pm. Hong Kong's huge floating restaurant with its fantastic décor has long been a tourist attraction. Fare is seafood and other Cantonese dishes, not hugely overrated, but a popular tourist experience. The restaurant offers a free sampan ride to its craft through the typhoon shelter and back again.

MACAU

Military Club $$$ *Av. da Praia Grande, 795, tel: 714000.* Open daily noon to 3pm and 7 to 11pm. The atmospheric dining hall of the 1870 Clube Militar de Macau, with its high ceilings and arched windows is a rare glimpse into the past. The extensive menu offers excellent Portuguese cuisine.

Fat Siu Lau $$ *Rua da Felicidade, 64, tel: 573580.* Open daily 11.30am to 11.30pm. Macau's oldest restaurant has been renovated in a modern art-deco style. The Macanese menu includes a traditional roast pigeon prepared according to a 90-year-old recipe. No credit cards.

O Porto Interior $$ *Rua do Almirante Sergio, 259B, tel: 967770.* Open daily noon to 3pm and 6 to 11.30pm. Located on the Inner Harbour and not far from the Maritime Museum, this restaurant is notable for its colonnaded façade and its walls covered with *azulejos* and carved wooden grilles. The carefully prepared Macanese dishes are an excellent value.

GUANGZHOU (CANTON)

Lian Xiang Lou $$ *67 Dishifu Lu, tel: 8181 3388.* This outstanding restaurant is located on an interesting older shopping street that has survived in Guangzhou's relentless new construction. The décor is elaborate and elegant, and the Cantonese dishes are simply delicious.

INDEX